ALL THAT IS SACRED IS PROFANED

A Pagan Guide To Marxism

Rhyd Wildermuth

ALL THAT IS SACRED IS PROFANED
A Pagan Guide to Marxism

This work CC-BY-NC-SA: Rhyd Wildermuth, 2019

You are free to redistribute this work in any form,
digital or print, for non-commercial purposes
Redistributions must carry this exact license
and must attribute original author

ISBN: 978-1-7325523-3-3

Layout, cover design, and publication by
GODS&RADICALS PRESS

bulk, wholesale and solidarity copies available

Contact us at distro@abeautifulresistance.com

Visit our website:
ABEAUTIFULRESISTANCE.ORG

Table of Contents

Why a Pagan Guide to Marxism?

Perhaps you've heard—*the earth is dying*.

Not the actual earth, though. It's doing fine, still spinning on its axis along its elliptical course around the sun. I mean the living things on the earth, the ones which "world" our earth. Forests incinerated in great conflagrations after long droughts, trees collapsing from strange diseases their aeons-long evolutionary adaptations cannot fight off. Species extinctions have become regular news, as have unheard-of heat waves, 1000-year floods happening every few years. Crop failures, pandemic illnesses in livestock, collapsing ice shelves, spreading deserts.

Maybe you've also heard the projections, the panicked warnings from scientists who'd otherwise become so good at not sounding panicked that it's really quite unnerving. Civilizational collapse around the corner, 10 or 20 or optimistically 50 years if we're lucky.

You've also maybe heard about the refugee children being locked in cages, the immigrants hauled from their homes in the middle of the night or attacked on the streets by groups of angry people demanding they "go home." The sudden rise of nationalist and fascist movements in Europe and the Americas, authoritarian populists installed by groundswell democratic elections fueled by fear, insecurity, and terror.

I'm going to guess you've heard all this already. And it's not a far stretch to presume you've also heard all the reports about the wealthy getting wealthier as cities swell with homeless people. Yet in the midst of all this climate and political chaos, there are new things to buy, new apps for our iGadgets and new media distractions to ease our fears and fill the coffers of the capitalists.

That's our world now. But another world's always been possible. If anything, another world is the only thing possible now, because capitalism has made this world impossible.

Paganism has always been about making another world possible. A world where forests exist for themselves, rather than for the toilet paper that can be manufactured from the trees that compose them.

A world where rivers are sacred because they are goddesses and gods, where plants teach their use to the dreaming witch and animals guide the shaman into how to be more human.

This Paganism, more correctly called animism, existed everywhere in the world before the coming of capitalism. In some places it still exists, never fully eradicated by the market imperative or the missionaries. In Europe it appeared to die earlier, assaulted by Empire and the Church centuries before the first factories broke the fingers of children and the backs of their parents. It had to be this way, you see; you couldn't have people worshiping land if you were going to turn it into property.

Ironically, the birth of capitalism resurrected Paganism in Europe, or a kind of Paganism. Most of the early resistance movements to capitalism (the Levelers, the Luddites, the Rebeccas, the Whiteboys) evoked Pagan gods and goddesses and claimed to take part in Pagan rites in the name of fighting against a monstrous system destroying what was left of the sacred.

And that's where we come to that other thing I am, a Marxist. While in the 20th century Marx's ideas were contorted by Lenin's (and later Stalin's) "scientific socialism," an autonomous current has always existed, one which fights capitalism not merely to repeat its mistakes but to put an end to its terrifying destruction of the natural world, including its destruction of human lives. And it's no surprise that this autonomous current has been held strongest by indigenous movements that have also kept true to their animist beliefs.

Can Marxism or Paganism save us? No. Nothing can. The capitalists are betting more credit, or new technology, or a sudden discovery of unlimited fuel or new planets might get them out of this mess. The idea that a savior, a god or hero or political platform might pop out of a stage and fix everything is anyway a capitalist (and before it, Calvinist) delusion.

So why a Pagan guide to Marxism? Because we need to know our history. We need to know how we got where we are, what we lost, where we lost it, and how that history isn't over—it's now. Animism reminds us what is sacred, and Marxism tells us how it became profaned. From both threads of knowledge perhaps you, dear reader, might learn how to right at least some of what has gone wrong. Because no one is coming to save us; we need to save ourselves together.

CHAPTER ONE:
An Introduction
To Capitalism

In this chapter, you'll be given a general overview of what capitalism is and how it functions as a social, economic, political, historical, and class system. You'll also be introduced to some basic concepts of Marxism, and also get a short introduction to Karl Marx himself.

What's Capitalism?

Before we talk about anything else, let's take some time to try to define capitalism. Let's start with a very simplistic definition first:

> *Capitalism is a way of organizing society in which a small group of people own most of the resources and the rest of the people have to work for them to gain access to those resources to survive.*

Contained in that very simple statement, though, are a lot of unanswered questions:
- Why do societies need to be organized?
- Who is doing the organizing?
- Why should a small group of people own everything?
- What does it even mean to own things?
- What does working for someone actually mean?
- Why do the rest of the people work for that small group of people, and why is their survival tied to working for them?
- Who decided on all this, anyway?

CHAPTER ONE

We call capitalism an economic system, but as you can see from that very short list of questions, **capitalism isn't just about the exchange of goods and services.** Also, it is not a neutral system; written into its very premise is political and social inequality, and without that inequality it cannot actually function.

Capitalism: A Social Relationship

So, an important thing to remember is that economic systems are not merely isolated systems: they cannot be separated from other aspects of human society. In fact, it is a foundational premise of Marxism that economics are **social relations**, and social relations determine both how we interact with each other and also how we see ourselves.

The easiest way to understand this concept is to think about your own relationship to your boss. I don't just mean your manager, but the person who writes your checks—the person who pays you. Even if you get along with them well, you will always interact with them differently than you would with a friend, a neighbor, a stranger, or a family member, because your boss has power over whether or not you can pay your rent and whether or not you get to eat this month.

SOCIAL RELATIONS: All the interactions human have with each other, how they relate to each other and how they see themselves as part of a social group.

While you'd be honest with a friend who asks how you're feeling or straightforward with a neighbor whose music is too loud at night, telling your boss honestly that you wish they paid you better or that you were late because you drank too much the night before could get you fired. And getting fired doesn't just mean losing your job: it can mean losing the roof over your head as well.

If you don't have a traditional boss and instead work for a large corporation with managers and a human resource department, consider how you relate to your manager. Again, even if you get along with them great, you will always have a sense that you cannot fully be yourself around them, because they have the power to determine whether or not you keep your job.

In both cases, the power that a manager or boss holds over you is that they can fire you. And unless you have savings, getting fired from a job is a really awful thing, because **if you don't have work you don't have money, and if you don't have money you can't buy food, pay rent or other bills, or really do much of anything in a capitalist society.**

This is just one example of how social relations are determined by economic systems. Because your ability to live the sort of life you want to live (and even to survive at all) is tied to your job, you are limited in the way you can relate to your boss or manager. You can only assert yourself or defend your dignity so far before you risk unemployment, and so your interactions (your social relations) are constantly determined, limited, and shaped by this economic reality.

Capitalism: A Political Relationship

In the questions I listed about capitalism, you'll notice several of them were political questions. For instance, "Why do societies need to be organized?" and "Who decided on this, anyway?"

Another foundational premise of Marxism is that **capitalism is a political relationship.** In fact, the title of Karl Marx's most famous work was *Capital: A Critique of the Political Economy (Das Kapital: Kritik der politischen Oekonomie)*. By political relationship we mean all the questions of power and governance that determine how we relate to each other (and as in social relations, how we are not allowed to relate to each other).

POLITICAL RELATIONS:
The ways that laws, governments, power, force, co-ercion, and violence influence what we do, what we cannot do, and how we interact with each other.

CHAPTER ONE

Here are a few real-life examples of how the economic system of capitalism is a political system:

• Workers at a factory go on strike after a co-worker loses an arm in a machine after working 12 hours without a break. They vow to block the entrance to the factory until the boss meets with them, but police show up and arrest them.

• A community activist group plants a community garden and sets up a small homeless camp with an outdoor soup kitchen in an overgrown lot. Even though that lot has been left empty for ten years, and they did a lot of work to clean it up, the owner of the land asks a judge to make them leave. The judge agrees and also fines the group for trespassing.

• An elderly family cannot pay the taxes on the house they have lived in since they married 60 years ago. The city evicts them and sells it to a developer who demolishes it and builds condos.

• A hipster couple trademarks a widely-known and decades-old folk remedy, and then sues everyone who makes the remedy for intellectual property infringement and wins.

• The leaders of a small African country try to protect poor farmers from international competition by banning imports of genetically-modified wheat and corn. The World Trade Organisation intervenes, setting such huge fines that the country would collapse unless the leaders accept the banned crops.

• Poor families notice a bad smell coming from the water in their faucets and believe it is because of local fracking by oil companies. One man films himself turning on the faucet and sparking a lighter next to the stream and it ignites. The oil company sues Youtube to get the video removed...and wins.

As you can see from these examples, a lot more than buying and selling goes into maintaining the capitalist system. **It is upheld, maintained, and enforced by political means.** The police, the courts, international trade organisations, and governments themselves are an important aspect of capitalist rule. Marxist theory is not just a criticism of bosses and the rich, but also of the State that supports it.

Capitalism: A Class System

Let's look again at the very simple definition of capitalism that I offered.

> *Capitalism is a way of organizing society where a small group of people own most of the resources and the rest of the people have to work for them to gain access to those resources to survive.*

You'll notice that there are two groups of people in this definition: the ones that "own most of the resources" and the ones that "have to work for them." These groups are called "classes," and in Marxism the two major classes of people are the **capitalists** (the bourgeoisie) and the **workers** (the proletariat). We'll go deeper into these concepts later, but for now it's very important to understand what I mean when I talk about each class.

First, the bourgeoisie or capitalist class. The word "bourgeoisie" in French literally means "city-dweller," but in a Marxist context it is used to describe **the people actually engaged in capitalist exploitation** (bosses, owners, managers, landlords, CEO's, etc.). So even if you're a far-right conservative construction worker who thinks capitalism is the best thing ever, *you're not actually a capitalist.*

CLASS SYSTEM: An arrangement of society where people are divided according to their position, status, or activity: for instance, nobles, clergy, and peasants; warrior, priest and farmer; master and slave, or worker and owner.

The workers or proletariat is the other main class. The word literally means "producers of offspring," but in Marxist terms it means **those who must earn a wage to survive**. So the far-right conservative construction worker I just mentioned is part of the proletariat, just like I am, you are, and probably almost everyone you know.

CHAPTER ONE

You're probably wondering about a third class that I haven't mentioned, the middle class. It's not actually a class that Marx talked about much, because in the 1800's it didn't really exist. It still doesn't really exist, either, or not the way that we are taught to believe it does in the United States and Europe.

Think about what you've been led to believe about the middle class. What really makes them different from other workers? Not much, really, especially when you compare a middle-class income to the wealth of your average capitalist. A middle-class worker still needs to work to survive (though what they need to survive is less than most of them think), and isn't getting rich off the work of others like a capitalist does.

PROLETARIAT (WORKERS)
The lower class of capitalist society. Those who must work for a wage in order to survive. This also includes the homeless, disabled, and others who cannot work but do not have wealth.

BOURGEOISIE (OWNERS):
Those who profit from the work of others and do not need to work for a wage in order to survive

So middle-class people are really just higher-paid members of the proletariat, with one difference. They're often paid more because they share the values of the capitalist class and take the side of the capitalists over other workers. In essence, they act as a "buffer" between the poor and the rich.

Marxists see the conflict between these two primary classes (the capitalists and the workers) as the defining tension in capitalist societies. While other conflicts certainly exist as well (religious, ethnic, political, etc.), **class is the only tension that derives from a material basis** (what you have or don't have) rather than artificial divisions based on beliefs, allegiances, or social constructs like nationality or race.

Class cuts across all the other divisions of humanity. Consider: a woman can be a homeless sex-worker or a banking executive. A Mexican can be a migrant farm laborer or the owner of a housekeeping service. A transgender or queer person can be a barista struggling to pay rent or the head of a small media empire.

However, you cannot be both a capitalist and part of the proletariat at the same time. The moment a rich person loses all their money and has to work for others to survive, they've switched classes, and the same goes for a person who grew up poor who later starts a company that employs hundreds of people.

While some are more likely to be capitalists (whites, men, straight people, etc.) **and others are more likely to be workers** (indigenous, Black, women, etc.), **class is a conflict within every group.** (This will be addressed in much greater detail in chapter four.)

Capitalism: A Historical System

Many people, especially in the United States, have trouble imagining that there was ever a time before capitalism. There are a lot of reasons for this, including decades of anti-communist propaganda in the schools and the media, as well as the sheer difficulty of imagining the past at all.

But it's true. **There was a time before capitalism, and as far as the history of humanity goes, that time wasn't very long ago at all.** Depending on how you date it, capitalism either started in the 1700's or the 1600's: when European nations transitioned from a system called feudalism. In chapter three we'll talk much more about this transition, but for our purposes now it's important to clear up some falsehoods you've probably been taught.

HISTORICAL SYSTEM: A system that can be traced to a specific time period and was created by "historical forces." For capitalism, those historical forces were the enclosure of the Commons in Europe and the accumulation of wealth through slavery and colonization of indigenous peoples in Africa, Asia, and the Americas.

• First of all, **capitalism and markets are not the same thing.** As far as we know, people have always exchanged things between themselves, often (but not always) using some form of common currency as a symbol for what was exchanged. But capitalism is not just markets and exchange: it's a social and political economic system where the only way for the majority of the world to participate in exchange is to work for others.

· The next point is related to that one. While there have always been times that people might choose to work for others, **within capitalism, most people (except the capitalists) have no choice but to work for others**. That doesn't mean it's necessarily slavery—almost no one goes to work with a loaded gun pointed at their head. But that's part of the power of capitalism, because unlike in slavery or feudalism, the rich don't need to use direct violence to make us work for them any longer. Instead, through several historical processes, the capitalists were able to convince people to not need a loaded gun.

· And the last point we need to be clear on: capitalism didn't just arise out of nothing. It was not a "natural" process, nor is it a naturally-occurring system. **Without direct intervention, constant force, violent repressions of revolts and rebellions, and perpetual propaganda from politicians and media, capitalism wouldn't be able to continue.** The proof for this in a brief glance at how much money the capitalists spend to make sure you spend money on their new products and how much governments spend to arrest and incarcerate those who break laws related to private property.

Capitalism: An Economic System

So we've looked at how capitalism is a political, social, and class relationship, and briefly touched upon its place in history, but we haven't actually looked at capitalism as an economic system.

First of all, what do we mean by economics? The classic definition is that economics is "the branch of knowledge concerned with the production, consumption, and transfer of wealth," and thus an economic system would be the ways production, consumption, and transfer of wealth occur.

Before looking at the economics of capitalism, let's break this definition into its three parts (production, consumption, and transfer of wealth) to make sure we understand what each means.

ECONOMICS: The management of production, consumption, and transfers of wealth. From the ancient Greek word *oikonomia*, which referred to household management. It was introduced into Modern society through the Catholic Church, which believed there was a God-ordained way that societies should be managed.

• **Production**: A cook prepares meals, a textile worker sews together fabric to make t-shirts, a computer programmer writes code to create an app, a migrant worker picks tomatoes, and a child-care worker takes care of children while their parents are at work: these are all types of production. Even if there is no physical product being produced, something is created or done that someone consumes.

• **Consumption:** A customer eats a meal at a restaurant, or buys a t-shirt, or eats a tomato...basically, people consume what other people produce.

• **Transfer of Wealth:** What's wealth? Well, in modern society, we think of wealth as money. But money is only a representation of wealth: you can have a million dollars, but if no one will take your money and there's nothing for you to buy, you just have a bunch of paper or some numbers in a computer. So wealth, then, is both the resources you have (land, money, goods) as well your ability to get things with that wealth (including more wealth). That's what the "transfer" of wealth means: how this wealth is moved around between people.

Now—those are the general concepts of all economic systems, but how do these work in capitalism?

• **Capitalist Production:** A cook prepares a meal at a restaurant where she works. She doesn't own the ingredients or the kitchen or the restaurant itself; instead, all of that belongs to the restauranteur who pays her to work in his restaurant. Similarly, the woman who sews together a t-shirt doesn't own the factory where she works, nor the fabric or the sewing machines she uses. The same with the coder who makes the app for a social media company, the migrant farmer who picks tomatoes on a large corporate farm, and the child care worker at a day care.

Though they all produce things, they don't actually own what they make or the places they work (the "means of production"). And not only that, they don't have the right to sell what they've made directly to consumers.

• **Capitalist Consumption:** When you buy an app for your phone or a meal at a restaurant, who do you pay? You don't pay the person who made it; instead, you pay the owner or a company. It's the same with tomatoes and t-shirts: you buy them at a store which bought them from a distributor who bought them from the farmer or t-shirt company. In capitalism, your consumption is always far removed from the actual production of the things you consume.

• **Capitalist Transfer of Wealth:** In capitalism, wealth is transferred upward (from workers to capitalists) by means of sales and rent, and transferred downward by means of wages (and to some degree by taxation). But this is never an equal movement: more wealth is always moved upwards than it is downwards, and so the rich get richer and the poor get poorer.

This happens because **in capitalist production, the means of production are owned by the capitalists and the prices for wages, rents, and items consumed are also controlled by the capitalists.** Neither the consumer nor the producer have any significant power or any real relationship at all; there is always an intermediary, the capitalist.

The Marxist View of Capitalism Vs. Other Views

Now that we've looked at the multiple aspects of capitalism, here's a more thorough answer than the one I provided at the beginning of this chapter.

> *Capitalism is an economic, social, and political system in which the means of production, consumption, and exchange are owned and controlled by a minority class of people, while the majority class of people must work for them in order to gain access to wealth through wages.*

This definition of capitalism is the Marxist definition. But here's a different definition, one more sympathetic to capitalism, from the Cambridge English dictionary:

> *an economic, political, and social system in which property, business, and industry are privately owned, directed towards making the greatest possible profits for successful organizations and people.*

You'll see that this definition also states that capitalism is a political and social system as well as an economic system. This fact is not disputed, even by the most ardent supporters of capitalism. As well, the definition states that "property, business, and industry are privately owned," which is also the Marxist definition. And one more thing: no Marxist would disagree that that those things are "directed towards making the greatest possible profits," either.

Here's another definition, from an investment dictionary:

> *Capitalism is an economic and social system in which participants privately own the means of production—called capital. Free market competition, not a central government or regulating body, dictates production levels and prices.*

Note that this definition excludes the word "political." It does, however, allow that capitalism is not just an economic system but also a social one.

In both of these definitions, you'll notice the word "privately" appears. **Private property is a crucial aspect of capitalism**, one that our simple definition also includes ("owned and controlled by a minority class of people...") All these definitions agree about the basic facts of capitalism. But if these definitions are all so similar in content, then why do they seem so different?

The reason for that difference is whom they include in the definition. Take a moment to look at both the Cambridge English dictionary definition and the investment dictionary definition and ask yourself, "where do I fit in to this definition?"

PRIVATE PROPERTY: A system in which land and resources are property that can be bought or sold. For instance, under capitalism land is private property, so only those who have money to buy land can raise their own food. Private Property does not refer to Personal Property (like clothing).

The truth is, you don't. Both definitions—and indeed almost all non-Marxist definitions—of capitalism describe what capitalism is like for the capitalists. The "participants" who "privately own the means of production" in the investment definition are the capitalist class, and no words are used to describe what capitalism is like if you are not a "participant." The same holds true for the Cambridge dictionary definition: "property, business, and industry are privately-owned," but by whom?

The core difference between the Marxist definition and other ones is that a Marxist framework asks, "what about the workers? They are, after all, the ones actually doing the production and consumption..." Non-Marxist definitions of capitalism exclude everyone except for the owners of property and production specifically because the owners are the only ones who actually control everything.

Workers, on the other hand, function as invisible and inter-changeable cogs in the machines that the capitalists run, much like all the factory workers who make a car or a smart phone are invisible to you when you purchase it, but the company (Ford, Apple) that "made" the item is not.

Marx's Dangerous Idea

We've spent the first 3000 words of this chapter talking about capitalism from a Marxist perspective, but we haven't really talked about Marxism much besides discussing a few core ideas. To re-iterate, we've learned so far that Marxism:

• Insists that economics are social relations, and social re-lations determine both how we interact with each other and also how we see ourselves.

• Insists that capitalism is a political relationship, supported and maintained by political institutions

• Sees the conflict between these primary classes (the capitalists and the workers) as the defining tension in capi-talist societies.

• Insists that capitalism was created by historical processes and can be located in history (rather than being eternal or ancient).

• Asks, "what about the workers?" in definitions of capital-ism.

If you were raised (like I was) to fear the ideas of Marx or to worry about communism taking over America, these things probably don't seem nearly as scary or as dangerous as what the media, schools, pastors, and politicians told you.

That, by the way, isn't just because much of their propa-ganda was wrong, since we haven't yet talked about the most dangerous part of Marxism. Marx and others who came after him don't just criticize capitalism—they offer a sugges-tion on what to do about it.

That's the dangerous part.

Marx and others argue that, if it's the workers actually doing all of the production and consumption, then they should be the ones who decide how its done and what they get paid for their work.

That simple idea is what has caused multiple revolutions, wars, beatings, assassinations, bombings, jailings, blacklistings, and many other violent acts in the last 200 years, both by those trying to enact Marx's idea and especially by those trying to make sure Marx's idea never comes to pass.

Karl Marx: The Alchemist

Here we need to be clear about something else. Karl Marx was absolutely not the first person to criticize capitalism or offer an alternative. From the very first moment that factories began springing up in Europe and at the sign of the very first land eviction during the Enclosures, people have been resisting capitalism. In fact, when Karl Marx and Fredrich Engels wrote *The Communist Manifesto* in 1848, there had been thousands of riots, work stoppages, protests, and organized resistances against this new system.

What Marx did do first, however, was to connect together everything that was happening across Europe as well as in the colonized lands outside Europe—all the economic and political exploitation as well as the earth-shaking societal changes—into a narrative that none had been able to see before.

Marx was not an economist by training (in fact, there weren't really economists yet). Rather, he was a philosopher and a journalist (for an American newspaper, by the way) who studied law and history. It was this varied background as well as his life experiences which brought him to an understanding of the way capitalism functioned throughout the world. And while an atheist, his writing has an esoteric, almost alchemical feel to it. In his writings, he speaks of the "crystallization" of value and speaks of labor as if it is a magical force of transmutation.

As far as anyone knows, Marx wasn't an alchemist, and no doubt his atheism makes it quite unlikely he ever would have considered the occult to be more than nonsense. Yet what Marx did is alchemy itself: combining apparently different and oppositional ideas and processes into a powerful narrative that still "haunts," as the opening of *The Communist Manifesto* says.

It's my opinion, however, that Karl Marx should be studied as one might study the works of renaissance magicians or ancient grimoires. As we delve further into what capitalism is, how it functions, what its affects are, and also what Marxism proposes, try to approach these ideas not only with the intellectual part of your understanding, but also the more emotive and magical parts of your being as well. In this way, you will find deep wells of connection between the horrors of capitalism and the "disenchantment of the world" that Pagans fight against.

Study Questions & Futher Reading

1. How does the definition of capitalism provided in the very beginning of the chapter differ from how you've heard it defined elsewhere?

2. We often hear talk of the "haves" and "have nots." How does that fit into this definition? And do you feel dividing society into two groups such as this is necessarily correct?

3. How does it feel to consider that there are limits to your relationships with people caused by capitalism? Can you think of other examples?

4. Every single one of the examples of how capitalism is also a political relationship were events which have actually occurred (and still do). We are often taught to think of government, police, and the judicial system as forces which protect our rights, but in those examples the "rights" being protected are the interests of capitalists. How does this change your current understanding of how governments work?

5. In many English-speaking countries, most people tend to think of themselves as "middle class," whether they make $200,000 a year or $20,000. Likewise, politicians and the media often bemoan the "shrinking middle class." How does the Marxist view of class change the way you see your own financial situation? And do you feel you have more in common with people poorer than you or richer than you?

6. Thinking about capitalism historically is a very difficult process. Oftentimes we are told that "this is the way it has always been." Why might this be? And what are the links between thinking of capitalism as having always been "the way things are" and our ideas of what is natural?

7. One criticism of economics in general and Marxism in particular is that economic theory seems to reduce life to production,

consumption, and exchange. From what you have read so far, do you think this is true?

8. In the examples of production, consumption, and exchange, describing the capitalist version shifted the focus away from the act itself towards the people involved. The next time you purchase or consume something, try to imagine the people who were involved in its production. Does this change your feeling about the item? And how might imagining these people relate to animism (the belief that everything has spirit)?

9. Related to the previous question, consider how the brand of an item (for instance, a smartphone or your shoes) relates to the way you experience the item. If you own an iPhone, for instance, is it easier to think about the people who assembled it or about Apple? Could there be an esoteric or occult dimension to brands?

Further Reading

LIGHT
For a rather amusing description of Karl Marx, read this detective report: https://medium.com/@muetricht/karl-marx-was-the-original-dirtbag-leftist-6ec6319545f3

A fairy-tale about capitalism and witchcraft: *The DisEnchanted Kingdom*: https://abeautifulresistance.org/site/2015/08/25/the-disenchanted-kingdom

MODERATE
The Roots of Our Resistance: https://abeautifulresistance.org/site/2015/05/29/the-roots-of-our-resistance

INTENSIVE
The Communist Manifesto: Introduction & Chapter One: https://www.marxists.org/archive/marx/works/1848/communist-manifesto/ch01.htm#007

CHAPTER TWO: The Basics of Capitalism

This chapter, we'll look at what capital is and how it functions. We'll also examine class and class conflict, particularly how capitalists work together as a class for their own interests. And we'll explore a little bit of how the government (the State) fits into capitalism.

What's The Owner Do Around Here, Anyway?

When you go to a restaurant, a lot goes into making the meal you eat at a table. Prep-cooks prepare the ingredients earlier in the day, cooks do the actual cooking and put it on a plate, servers take your order and bring out the food, bussers clean your table, and dishwashers wash everything that was used (and usually clean up the restaurant at the end of the night.

What's the restaurant owner do? Well, they write the checks, do the advertising, pay the bills, hire the workers, pay everyone according to the wages they set, and at the end of the day take home the extra. Why does the restaurant owner get to take home the extra? Well, because he's the owner.

Why does he own the place, though? Well, because he had money to start with. It takes a lot of money to start a restaurant, to buy all of the equipment, rent the building, put in tables and chairs, and then to buy the initial ingredients that will be used to make the food.

So the fact that a restaurant owner started out with money is what allows them to earn more money. And the fact that the workers in the restaurant didn't start out with money is what makes them have to work for the restaurant owner.

That's capitalism.

But what if the workers owned the restaurant instead? What if they got to decide how much everyone got paid, managed the restaurant together, set the working conditions and the prices? What if they got to split the extra profit that was made at the end of the day?

That would be communism.

Capital & The Means of Production

When a person has a large sum of money that they then use to start a business, we call that money "capital." And the business that they run? We call that **the means of production**. And when they hire other people to work at their business? We call them them a **capitalist**.

A capitalist, then, is someone who has used their capital to acquire the means of production, and then employs people to produce for them. Whether or not they also work at the business (many restaurant owners do) is besides the point: the key to being a capitalist is paying others to work your capital for you. And in capitalism, the best (and really the only) way to get capital is to already have capital.

Let's look at the concepts I've introduced in these paragraphs a little closer. First, I'll give you a short definition of each, and then I'll give you more examples of how they play out.

As mentioned in the previous chapter, it's a good idea to approach these concepts not just with your intellectual understanding, but the more magical and emotive ways of knowing as well.

Capital is money that is used to make more money. At the time of this writing, I have 85.20 US dollars in my bank account. That's not capital, because I am not using it to make money. If, however, I used that money to buy a table, some lemons, and some sugar for the purpose of making lemonade and selling it, that money becomes capital.

So, capital is a category of wealth, not wealth itself. It's what's being done with the wealth that makes it capital or not. It's a bit like the difference between groceries and dinner, or plants and vegetables. Dinner is what was done with the groceries you bought, vegetables are a category of plants that are eaten in a certain way.

The means of production are all the resources required to produce things. Examples of the means of production are: factories, stores, restaurants, workshops, offices, and hair salons, but also tools, printers, copy machines, kitchens, computers, knitting needles and yarn, and any other implement you might need to make something.

When Marxists speak of the means of production, they are also usually talking about the larger systems that enable exchange as well as production: for instance, internet service providers, shipping and distribution networks, e-commerce websites, and even credit card processors and banks are also part of the means of production.

What's production, then? It's all the activity humans engage in to make things that they use or exchange with each other. When I make myself dinner, I am engaging in production, just like as I type this for you to read I am producing something. **Production is what we create, our acts of creation.** Without

CAPITAL:
Wealth that is used to make more wealth. This can include money invested to build a factory or restaurant. Capital is not the same as money or wealth, but a way that money or wealth is used.

THE MEANS OF PRODUCTION
The resources required to produce something. For instance, land, farming tools, water, and seeds are all needed to grow food, so all those things are the means of production of food.

PRODUCTION:
All that acts that humans do in order to create things, and the things they create.

the means of production, we are limited in what we can create. Without this laptop, I cannot create a textbook for you to read; without a stove, I can't cook dinner.

A Basic Example

Now, let's look at how capital and the means of production work together.

A family has a small plot of land. They work it themselves, and don't hire anyone to help them. That family isn't capitalist, even if they sell the extra they produce.

In fact, that's the basic mode of economic activity most lower class people (peasants, serfs, etc.) have engaged in since the birth of agriculture itself. They grew and made what they needed, and then exchanged anything extra (their "**surplus production**") with others for anything else they needed.

SURPLUS PRODUCTION: What is created above what the person who created it uses or needs. This extra is either shared, or traded in exchange for the surplus of others.

Like a restaurant, that farm (and all the farming equipment, seeds, etc.) are the means of production. The family who has that land, therefore, has access to their own means of production. They can produce things on their own terms, can decide what to do with what they produce, can determine what to do with any money they get from selling the extra (their surplus production) that they don't use themselves. So, they don't just have access to the means of production, they control their own production.

Now, let's say that family hires someone to work the farm for them. Let's name this person Juan, because in North America, the vast majority of farm workers are migrant workers from Mexico and other countries who have no wealth of their own. The family pays Juan some money to do some or all of the work for them: water their crops, weed, and pick vegetables when they are ripe. Juan is now doing production for the family, and when all the vegetables and fruit are picked, they sell the extra and give Juan some of the money.

That family? They're now capitalists. Their farm, which is a means of production, is now also their capital. They use it (and Juan) to make money by selling all the vegetables that Juan grew for them that they don't eat themselves (Juan's surplus production).

They are able to do this because Juan doesn't have his own farm. Juan is poor, and Juan wants to eat just like everyone else, so Juan works for the family in return for some money that he then uses to buy food and other things he needs.

What is really the difference between the family and the workers they hire? It's quite likely the workers know just as much about farming—and maybe even more—than the owners of the farm. And farming is a lot of work, and Juan and others are doing most (and sometimes all) of it.

So why does Juan have to work for the family and not the other way around? Because the farmer has the land and Juan does not. That land is capital, and the farm is the means of production of food. When Juan works for the farmer, he is producing food for the farmer but not producing it for himself.

Labor

When Juan works for the farm owners to produce for them, we call the work that he does **labor**.

Just like capital is functional category of wealth (what it's being used for), labor is a sort of work. It is work that, when applied to something, adds value to the thing. It's not a far stretch to say that labor is work that is endowed with magical, transformative power, and it's a crucial foundation of Marxism that we are "alienated" from our labor (more on that later).

A simple way of thinking about labor is this. Consider what happens when a potter takes a lump of raw clay and shapes it into a ceramic vase. Without her skill, attention, artistic ability, and previous education and experience, the raw clay would remain raw clay and could never become a vase. Also, the amount that others will appreciate a vase (the amount they'll value it) is much higher than people will value a lump of clay.

LABOR
Work that is applied to resources in order to create something from it. Labor is what transforms clay into pottery, ingredients into dinner, stone into a house, or knowledge into an essay

All the things they might use a vase for, the way its design and colors make them feel, the way it might inspire them in floral arrangements—that value was only made possible by the labor of the potter.

Now, the same process that occurs when a potter turns clay into a vase is what happens all the time—it's what we humans do. The chef who cooks a meal from raw ingredients has used his labor to make a meal, just like the dishwasher at the end of the night applies her labor to turn dirty plates into clean plates.

When we apply our labor to something, we change it, shape it, create things from it, and generally add value and meaning to the world.

This transformative power of labor is what a capitalist requires to turn their capital into more capital. A rich woman can build a restaurant, decorate it beautifully, advertise it everywhere, and buy all the best quality ingredients in the world, but until she has people to work in it, she cannot make any money. A rich man might have a hundred acres of forest, but until he has labor to cut down the trees and turn it into toilet paper for him, he cannot make any money from the trees.

Capital and Dead Labor

Labor is the animating magic of capitalist production, the ghost in the machine or the spirit in the golem. And though it might seem a little strange to talk about it in magical terms, to do so is following an example set by Marx himself. Consider the following quote from Marx:

The Basics of Capitalism

Capital is dead labor, which, vampire-like, lives only by sucking living labor, and lives the more, the more labor it sucks.

This quote from *Capital* (volume 1) is from a section where he speaks about what he calls the "Organic Composition of Capital." While his entire theory is much more complex than we have space for in this course, the quote about dead labor and vampires explains much of the idea already.

If a capitalist employs labor to turn his capital into more capital, than it follows quite simply that the capital he earns is derived from the labor of others. **But what about the capital he starts with? Well, often enough, that was created by labor too.**

Let's look at the restaurant example. When a person opens a restaurant, they usually hire people to turn an empty space into something more suitable for their business. So, builders come in and tear out walls, install tiles and sinks and ovens in the kitchens, paint the walls, build a bar, and do many other things to make a restaurant. All of that is labor, which then creates more capital (the restaurant) that functions as a site of food production. And of course, all the wood and tile and wires the builders use and install came from somewhere: from other laborers, employed by other capitalists, often in factories that were also built with labor.

But what about the restaurant owner herself? Where did she get the money to do all of this? In each case it's different, but often enough she was probably born with some degree of wealth or had access to ways of getting more (through loans). If she was born with wealth, her parents probably got it from labor (and likely not their own). If she received a loan to open a business, the bank got that money from people who got it from labor.

The important thing to remember here is that all capital comes from human labor at some point. Whether it's the capital that corporations use now (some of it from slave labor hundreds of years ago) or the lemonade a child sells at a stand (someone had to pick those lemons), human labor was somewhere involved. Even products made completely by robots are made with human labor, because humans were involved in building those robots. There is no capital without human labor.

Value and the Alienation of Labor

As I said above, labor is really the animating magic of capitalism, the organic composition of everything the capitalist does. As a sort of human magic which transforms the world, our labor-power is an integral part of our existence.

It's how we create things of value. **But since we're all living in capitalist societies, our idea of value is dominated by the logic of the market—what can be bought and sold, and for how much.**

Say I invited you over for dinner. I go gather ingredients—meat and cheese and vegetables from the weekly open-air market, greens and herbs from my garden, bread from a baker, and maybe wine or cider. Then, I combine these ingredients, cook some of them, rinse and slice others, warm the bread in the oven, and then put it all on plates as you arrive. We then eat together and have a wonderful evening of conversation.

VALUE
What a thing is considered to be "worth." The concept of value extends into the far Pagan past, when a thing or a person was said to have value because it reflected an aspect of the gods. Value was once thought to be intrinsic (inherent to a person or thing). In modern capitalism, however, value (the worth of a thing or person) is determined by the market, by how much someone is willing to pay for it.

I have created something of value for you from my labor, but of course I'm not charging any money. In fact, we don't think of money at all, and just enjoy ourselves.

That enjoyment is what is meant by value, or what used to be meant by value before capitalism came to dominate our lives. Now, value is what we think items have: how much a dinner costs you to purchase at a restaurant is its value, instead of the experience itself.

Now, the labor I put into making that meal (and all the labor that went into growing the food in the first place) is what gave it value. I'm a great cook, and find cooking to be a lot like magic. (If we think of labor as a kind of human magic, then I'm not wrong in this!)

If I were doing this all in a restaurant, and you were just customers of the restaurant and I was getting paid to cook for you, I won't get the same sort of pleasure cooking the meal. In fact, cooking would feel a lot less like magic and a lot more like work.

The way that the feeling of human magic seeps out of our labor in such instances is part of what Marx called **"Alienation of Labor."** Our labor in such circumstances doesn't feel like it's ours anymore. In a way, it isn't: we've sold it to our employers in exchange for a wage.

And the things we create for our boss that have value? They aren't ours to share with others—they now belong to the capitalist who gets to sell them for his or her profit.

We'll look at Alienation of Labor again later, as the idea is a little more complex than this. One thing to keep in mind for now is that this alienation doesn't just mean we feel detached from our labor when we sell it. It means also that we completely forget that our labor was ever a part of us in the first place, and forget that what we purchase from others is also the product of labor.

> **ALIENATION OF LABOR**
>
> Under capitalism, we do not get to experience the direct benefit of our labor and instead receive wages. This leads to the sense that labor isn't a part of us, that we have no control over our creative powers, or even that labor is something we ever can have control over.

Wages and Labor

The capitalist needs labor to function, to make more capital. Without labor, the capitalist can do nothing with their capital.

CHAPTER TWO

But what motive does a worker have to sell their labor to a capitalist? A capitalist gets to earn more capital out of the exchange, but what does a worker get?

They get a **wage**, and that wage is how they eat. Without a wage, they can't eat, so the choice is pretty obvious: work or starve.

When I go to work for someone else, they offer to pay me a wage in return for my labor. A capitalist needs labor in order to gain more capital (profit), and because slavery is currently illegal in most of the world, in general the only legal means for him to get labor is to pay wages.

There are two ways to look at wages. The first, which is the most common non-Marxist way to look at them, is that wages are money that capitalists pay workers in return for the work they do. In this view, wages are just another cost that owners have to pay, similar to electric bills and rent.

In the Marxist view, wages are the price owners pay to purchase labor.

How much a capitalist will pay a person for their labor is determined by many factors, including the supply of available labor, the demand for labor, and governmental influence in the form of minimum wage laws. We'll look at each in turn, but first we must keep in mind that there is a primary hard and fast rule that sets an upper limit on the price a capitalist will pay pay for labor: **a capitalist will always pay a worker less than the value that worker created with their labor.**

WAGES
The price owners pay to purchase labor.

To understand this limit, we'll need to do some math.

• Let's say a man starts a small pottery studio and hires a potter to make vases for him. The potter makes 30 vases a month, and the owner sells each of them for $100. So, every month he takes in $3000 from sales of her vases.

• Now, let's say the costs to keep the pottery studio running (electricity, equipment, rent, insurance, clay, glazing, and all the other parts of the production) each month are $1000. So the pottery studio owner has $2000 left every month after all that.

 • Of course, there's one more cost we haven't mentioned yet: the potter herself. Slavery isn't legal, so the owner has to pay her, too. He's got $2000 left—how much will he pay her?

 • The answer is always less than $2000. Because if he pays her all of those profits, then he can't make any money himself.

REVENUE FROM VASE SALES: $3000
"OVERHEAD" COSTS: $1000
TOTAL PROFIT CREATED BY POTTER: $2000
WAGE TO POTTER: LESS THAN $2000

But remember, he's actually not making the vases, she is. So even if he pays her $1999 and only keeps $1 of it, he's made a profit off his capital (the studio itself) from her labor. No good capitalist would pay a worker that high of a share of the profits, however. Instead, her pay would likely be only $1000, with the owner pocketing the extra.

Within capitalism, this is considered completely normal and fair because it's the owner's shop after all, the potter only works there.

The $1000 the owner pays the potter is called a wage. It's the price he pays for her labor, and he needs that labor because he cannot or doesn't want to make the vases himself. The potter, on the other hand, doesn't have her own studio, so she needs to sell her labor to the owner in order to use her labor to get money to live.

Wages and Alienated Labor

The primary conflict within capitalism—the core engine of **class conflict**—comes from the fact that an owner and a worker have competing interests. A worker always wants to gain the most amount of reward possible from their labor, while a capitalist always want to gain the most amount of profit from their capital.

CHAPTER TWO

Take the example of the potter again. She makes beautiful vases, really enjoys making them, and feels most fulfilled when she creates them. It's all she ever wanted to do since she first took a ceramics class in school, and when she landed this job at the pottery studio, she was thrilled.

There's one problem. It doesn't really pay the bills. Her rent alone is $600 a month, and what's left over is only enough to pay utilities. She has to eat a lot of peanut butter sandwiches and packaged noodles just to make what's left over stretch until the next paycheck. Occasionally, she asks the owner for a raise, but he always sighs sadly and tells her there isn't enough money right now.

CLASS CONFLICT
The tension between the working class and the capitalist class caused by their competing interests. Workers want the highest value possible from their labor and therefore high wages, capitalists want the highest profit from their capital and therefore low wages.

When one day the owner accidentally leaves his business journal out on a desk and she learns how much he's making, she's feels sick to her stomach. He's making as much as she is, but she's the one who's doing all the work.

Now, let's look at things from the owner's perspective. Let's say the studio is his only form of income. He's also only making $1000 a month, and he's constantly worried that he'll have a bad month of vase sales and make even less. He wishes he could pay the potter more—he knows she's not eating well, and he really likes her work. But if he paid her more, he'd earn less. And besides, it was his investment in the first place that made the studio.

On days when she asks for a raise, he reminds himself that he's taking all the risk: all the potter has to do is show up, make vases, and collect a paycheck.

There's a chance that these two scenarios sound equal. I've purposefully written them so they will seem that way, because this is how they are presented to us in the narrative of capitalism. In fact, every small business owner I've ever

The Basics of Capitalism

worked for (I worked in a lot of restaurants before I became a writer) was quick to point out how much risk they took on, how uncertain the business climate was, how little money was left over. Sometimes they told the truth, most of the time they lied, but always their initial answer was "no."

Owners wish to keep wages as low as possible while still having people to work for them, and workers want as much money as possible from the work they are doing.

Fortunately for the owner (and unfortunately for us), there are plenty of external mechanisms (like the State) that favor the capitalist in such conflicts. We'll look at those in the next section, but there's one primary thing which is always in the capitalist's favor that has nothing to do with police or laws.

That thing? Our alienation from our own labor. Without alienation from labor, the balance of power is on the side of the worker

If in the scenario of the pottery studio the potter were to quit, the owner wouldn't just lose a worker, he'd lose his profit and his capital (remember: the sales from her labor aren't just paying for her wages and his own livelihood but also the rent on the studio itself). He has more to lose than she does in any conflict, and so if it looks like she is going to quit, he would be likely to accede to her demands.

It was the same in every negotiation I ever had with restaurant owners. Because I knew that without my labor the restaurant owner couldn't continue to make money, I could time my demand at the beginning of a very busy night (like Valentine's Day, for instance) and threaten to leave if the owner didn't agree. Facing the possibility of losing the labor required to make money, the owner would give me my requested raise.

Capitalists rely on our feeling of disconnection from our own labor-power. When we do not see the connection between the labor we do for them and their need of our labor to make money, they can keep our wages low.

CHAPTER TWO

But that isn't to say that the fault for low wages is on the workers alone. Much more goes into our alienation from our own labor than just our own recognition, including capitalist manipulation of the labor market. Times of high unemployment, for instance, make it easier for capitalists to find more workers to replace those who demand higher wages, while also making it riskier for workers to make those demands.

But there are also more violent means capitalists can use to keep wages low.

Capitalists And The State

Capitalism is not just an economic system but also a political system. Laws, courts, judges, police, prisons, the military, and other parts of the **State** all have parts to play within capitalism, and almost all of the State's influence favors the capitalists, not the workers.

Let's return to Juan, who is doing all the work on a farm. If Juan decides he wants better pay and the farm owners say no, one option available to him is just to leave the farm completely during harvest season. All the crops would rot and the farm owners would make no profit that year.

But there's a problem. Juan can't just leave the farm, because he's an undocumented immigrant. If he leaves, he's afraid that the owners will report him to immigration authorities who will arrest, imprison, and then deport him back to Mexico. In fact, the risk for deportation is so severe for him that he will probably never ask for a raise in the first place, and maybe won't even say a word when the farm owners pay him less than they promised.

And what about the potter? Remember that she really, really loves making pottery...it was her life's dream. Because

THE STATE
The government, including all its institutions, laws, and officials. So, politicians, judges, police officers, tax officials, prisons, courts, the military, and all of the laws they create and enforce. Capitalists rely on these laws and institutions to protect their interests.

the owner won't give her a raise, she comes up with the idea of sneaking into the studio late at night and making vases for herself that she can then sell and take all the profit from. She even tries to be as honest as possible about it and buys her own clay so she's not stealing.

But one night her boss catches her, realises that his customers might buy directly from her instead, and forces her to sign a non-compete agreement in order to be allowed to continue working for him.

In both of these cases, **the capitalist has access to an external political means of getting the upper hand over their workers**. But what kind of access does a worker have? Not much, at least from the State. The undocumented worker (especially in the United States) cannot just call the police on a farm owner who didn't pay him wages. Likewise, the potter cannot ask the government to make the owner give her a raise.

While many governments have some laws protecting workers from certain abuses by owners, these are very often nothing compared to the laws protecting owners. Even in countries with very strong labor protections (as in France), when workers make revolutionary demands on owners, the government will often send out the police and military to protect the owners, not the workers.

If it seems to you that the State and the capitalists collude together against workers, you're starting to think like Marx did. However, this goes against one of the primary arguments for capitalism offered by its strongest proponents: neoliberals, American libertarians (also called free-market libertarians, or Right Libertarians), and conservatives. All three see governments as a potential enemy to free-markets and capitalist activities, and assert that the less a government interferes with the economic activity of the people, the more free the people will be. (This idea is often called "laissez-faire" economics, which means "leave it to happen" in French).

CHAPTER TWO

Labor and the State

At this point you might be wondering: what about government-guaranteed worker protections? If you are in the United States, for instance, you might be thinking of minimum wage laws or the regulations that local, state, and federal governments put in place to make sure a boss cannot force you to work without pay or breaks. Doesn't this mean government is also on the side of workers?

The answer to this is that **the government can sometimes be on the side of the workers, but only when they are forced to be.** Recently, France saw one of its largest transportation strikes in history. There were traffic jams of up to 400 kilometers long entering Paris, train stations were so packed that people fell onto the tracks, and airports ground to a halt. All of these actions happened because the government of Emmanuel Macron attempted to loosen the protections that transportation-sector employees have. Those protections were put in place decades ago because of similar strikes and other pressures from workers.

The same is true in the United States: the 40 hour work week, minimum wage laws, and government protections of workers did not happen just because governments merely chose to pass them. They were forced to put them in place by pressure from organized workers.

When workers organize together to go on strike (or even to vote in one bloc in an election), they are acting together as a class. This is what is part of what is meant by class consciousness: workers recognizing mutual interests with other workers as a group, while at the same time recognizing that they have opposing interests with capitalists.

Capitalists Compete, Capitalists Collude

Capitalists also have class consciousness. That is, they often act together to suppress worker protections, even though capitalists are generally in competition with each other.

The Basics of Capitalism

Capitalists generally don't like government restrictions on their activities: they argue that these restrictions make it harder for them to do business. For the most part, they are correct. Regulations such as minimum-wage laws, overtime pay, maternity leave, and health-and-safety requirements all increase the cost a capitalist must pay to buy labor from workers.

If the potter we spoke about earlier were to become pregnant, and if the laws in the country she lives in required her employer to pay wages to her for several months while she gives birth and nurses her baby, that means the owner of the pottery studio not only will lose money while she is not working but also must find someone else to replace her temporarily, otherwise his production shuts down.

Minimum wage laws likewise make business difficult for a capitalist. **Remember: the capitalist always wants to pay the least amount possible for labor, while the worker wants to get the most amount possible for their labor.**

We've seen already that there is an absolute maximum that an owner is willing to pay for labor: they'll never pay the full amount they earn from a worker's labor, otherwise they cannot profit. But without external pressure (either from workers acting together as a class or from government restrictions put in place due to demands from workers), any individual owner has no lower threshold except what a worker is willing to accept.

We can see this problem best in Juan's situation. Since Juan is an undocumented worker and thus isn't protected by minimum wage laws, and because Juan is terrified of being imprisoned for being in the country illegally, there isn't much stopping the farm owner from paying Juan nothing at all except Juan himself.

CLASS CONSCIOUSNESS
When those of a class (either the working class or the capitalist class) set aside other differences to act together on their shared interests, as part of a class. For workers, this can mean setting aside other differenes and going on strike; for capitalists, this often means colluding to lower wages and benefits to workers.

CHAPTER TWO

If one day the owner says to Juan, "I'm not paying you for the rest of the year, and if you try to leave I'll call Immigrations and Customs Enforcement," Juan doesn't really have any good choices left to him. If he leaves, he'll go to jail. If he stays, he has to work for free.

This, by the way, is **slavery**, which we'll look at in more depth when we study the history of capitalism. For now, it's only important to keep in mind that **the choices of a worker are ultimately determined by the owners, and when owners act as a class, those choices are even more limited.**

Even if Juan could go to another farm instead, it's likely that farmer will give him the same ultimatum. Why? Because if one capitalist gets away with paying workers nothing, then that capitalist will be more profitable than all the other capitalists. A farmer whose labor cost is zero can sell his vegetables for less than what other farmers can, yet still make the same (or more) profit.

Because people prefer to buy cheaper vegetables, they'll buy from that farmer, making him more successful and the other farmers less successful.

So even though capitalists are in competition with each other, they act together as a class to keep wages as low as possible by responding to each other's actions. A different example is the way that in America, large discount department store chains like Walmart and Target force their workers to show up earlier and earlier on Thanksgiving each year. Because those two chains are in competition with each other, when one decides to open at noon on Thanksgiving, the other does the same.

SLAVERY

A system or condition of coerced labor where the worker receives no compensation and cannot easily escape the situation.

They don't merely respond to each other, however. Capitalists also organize together in their mutual self-interest. Farm owners, again, are a primary example of this: they form political alliances (lobbying or industry groups) to demand the government let them set their own wages for agricultural labor.

The Basics of Capitalism

It may seem initially surprising, but agricultural industry groups (including owners of food processors, slaughter-houses, and similar industries), along with restaurant and hotel owners, are the single largest political group arguing against the arrest, imprisonment, and deportation of undocumented ("illegal") immigrants. The reason for this is simple: all these industries rely on sub-minimum waged labor for their profits. Without a ready supply of undocumented workers, they would have to pay better wages and thus would earn less profits. But at the same time, they never fully lobby for immigrants' freedom, because without some degree of fear that the government will deport them, undocumented immigrants might demand higher wages.

These are some of the ways that capitalists manipulate the labor market and keep wages low for workers, ensuring they have a steady and cheap supply of labor. And it's important to keep in mind that, while there are plenty of kind-hearted, socially-conscious people who are capitalists, because they rely on labor and must compete with other capitalists in order to profit, they contribute to this same manipulation regardless their morals.

Many of the restauranteurs for whom I worked were kind and caring people in everything they did...except payroll. Not because they wanted to see me have to take on another job or not go to the doctor because I couldn't afford it, but because their profit was at stake.

CAPITALIST EXPLOITATION OF IMMIGRANTS

The plight of undocumented immigrants within capitalism is particularly difficult. On the one hand, they are used by the capitalists to reduce overall wages because they are more willing to accept work at low wages. On the other hand, they are used by the capitalists to divide the workers: immigrants get blamed for unemployment and low wages. But Marxists insist that it is not the immigrants who are to blame, but the capitalists who exploit them.

CHAPTER TWO

Study Questions &
Further Reading

1. This chapter introduces a lot of economic concepts that may have been unfamiliar to you before. Or just as likely, you may have heard of these concepts but not understood them in this way. For each of the following concepts, try to define them in your own words.
   - Capital
   - Production
   - Labor
   - Value
   - Wages

2. Capital and labor are both functional categories of other things (wealth and work). How does this functional categorization relate to the way we tend to see certain aspects of magical practice? For instance, how does wine become an offering, a drawing become a glyph, or specific actions become part of a spell or ritual?

3. Though we haven't discussed it directly, you've probably already heard the phrase "seize the means of production." What do you think this means? What would it require?

4. The idea that labor is a magical aspect of human work is hinted at throughout Marx's works, but because he was an atheist (as have been many subsequent Marxist theorists), at no point is this ever directly stated and is my own unique interpretation. Do you find it helpful to look at labor in this way? And if so, might there be other places where a more magical or esoteric understanding of these concepts are useful?

5. Regarding the matter of "dead labor" (Marx's "organic composition of labor"): how does such a concept change the way you look at the items you consume or the tools you use to make things? And how might this relate to ancestral veneration?

6. With words like "value" that have both economic and non-economic meanings, it's often difficult to tell which meaning came

The Basics of Capitalism

first or to separate their economic uses from their non-economic uses. Think of other words like this, and see if you can trace how the capitalist/economic meaning of the word hides the older meanings of those words.

7. If you are currently working for a wage (whether salaried or hourly), see if you can guess how much more your labor is actually worth (how much value you create) to your employee than what they are paying you for. (As a general rule, most small businesses cap their payroll expenses at 33%, while larger corporations generally pay no more than 10-15% of their total budgets on wages, so multiply your wage before taxes by at least 3).

8. In what ways do you feel you've been alienated from your labor? What are some steps you might take now to help you reclaim this power of yours?

9. Many Marxists and anarchists disagree with Liberals on how useful the State is in helping workers get better wages and protections. Do you currently feel its possible to get the government "on your side" in these struggles? If so, what steps would be needed to make this happen? And if not, what should happen instead?

10. Oscar Wilde, in his essay "The Soul of Man Under Socialism," says that the logic of capitalism degrades both the souls of the poor and the rich. If this is true, how would you go about convincing a capitalist that they are worse off as capitalists?

Further Reading

Light:
"Marxist Business Consulting," from Existential Comics. http://existentialcomics.com/comic/136
Moderate
The Revolutionary Dead: Karl Marx, Part one:
https://abeautifulresistance.org/site/3078
Intensive
Oscar Wilde's essay, The Soul of Man Under Socialism
https://www.marxists.org/reference/archive/wilde-oscar/soul-man/

CHAPTER THREE:
The Birth & History
of Capitalism

In this chapter we'll look at how capitalism came about and how certain historical forms and forces shaped its birth.

This is the most important part of this book and introduces many potentially difficult concepts, so please be patient with yourself as you read it!

History As Progress or History As Process?

Before we look deeply into the roots of capitalism and the way it was born into the world, we need to have a brief discussion about history itself.

As people who live in capitalist societies, who have only ever known capitalism, we tend to accept the idea that history is a progression from lower or less complex states of existence towards higher or more complex states. Also, we make value-judgments about those states of existence: more complex and modern is "better," while simpler and older is "worse."

Try a thought experiment with me. Imagine what daily life looked like 500 years ago in what we now call France. Try to put yourself in the place of the average peasant (not a lord or lady). Imagine what you might be doing every day. Picture what you might be wearing and eating, where you might live, what your family looks like. Imagine what it's like to work, what sort of activities you do every day, and what it feels like afterward.

Now also try to sense that world—what it feels like, what it smells and tastes like, what sounds you hear when you wake and go to sleep.

How did you feel about this image? What kind of judgments may have come into your head? Did you cringe a little when I asked about "smell," perhaps imagining the reek of animal dung, body odor, rotting teeth, or other unpleasant things? Did you perhaps imagine yourself tired, sick from illnesses that couldn't be treated back then, exhausted from the relentless work of farming, sewing, and doing all the other things required to survive? Did you maybe imagine yourself bored, with nothing to read or watch, no internet or smartphone or even music to listen to whenever you wanted?

If you had negative feelings about what life might have been like, you are hardly alone. In fact, this is the dominant capitalist conception of what life was like before our modern era, and is what is quite often depicted in films and television. Life back then, according to this image, was "poor, nasty, brutish, and short."

What if I told you that this way of looking at the past is as new as capitalism itself?

Societies before ours, and even some societies that exist now, don't think of the past as a place where we were all miserable. In fact, there are some cultures that do not or didn't have a conception of "past" at all—what came before and what will come were more like places on a map or parts of a house. They were locations, not moments that have

THE DARK AGES

The Dark Ages was the term used to describe the period between the Fall of Rome and the beginning of the Renaissance in Italy. It was named this way in the 1600's by a Christian theologian, Petrarch, who claimed there was no writing being done and no knowledge discovered during that period. This is, in fact, untrue, but most of the discoveries were being done by Pagans, Jews, and Muslims so they didn't count in his estimation.

disappeared completely because they no longer occur.

Much of the reason why we look at the past as we do now comes from a particular worldview that arose in Europe through a mix of Christianity, "The Enlightenment," and Capitalism itself. For instance, the words I quoted above ("poor, nasty, brutish, and short") come from a 17th century Enlightenment philosopher named Thomas Hobbes: he is one of the people who helped create this conception of the past in the first place.

The "Progress Narrative"

I'll call this general conception of history (where the past is worse than the present) the **"Progress Narrative."** In this view of history, the present is always "better" than the past because it is more complex and more civil. Those who lived in that past might not have meant to be brutish and backward, but they had little choice because they were not yet enlightened. The ancient world was full of "superstition" and "primitive" ways of thinking, institutions like human sacrifice and slavery, and people lived in a kind of intellectual darkness. On the other hand, the present is better because we've "progressed" beyond all those ideas and institutions. We've collectively "seen the light" (the Enlightenment) and therefore live in superior, advanced cultures.

If this idea sounds a little Christian or imperialist, you're not wrong—Thomas Hobbes and other Enlightenment thinkers like him were indeed Christian, and they provided the primary moral and intellectual foundation for European colonization of the rest of the world.

THE ENLIGHTENMENT
Also called "The Age of Reason," the Enlightenment supposedly meant the end of the "dark ages" and the beginning of a new era of knowledge. But though many of our ideas about freedom and rights come from this period, many of the same thinkers who iterated them advocated for slavery, the colonization of foreign lands, racial ideology, and capitalism.

Others, such as Adam Smith (whose concept of the "invisible hand of the market" is oft-quoted by defenders of capitalism) also saw the past as something to be disgusted by and capitalism something to be embraced, especially because capitalism was constantly "improving" the way humans produced, consumed, and exchanged.

The "Process Narrative"

A different way of looking at history exists, one that Marx and Engels proposed. In this view, history should be seen as a process or series of processes. This is called historical materialism, or Marxist dialectical materialism. But rather than chasing one of the most confusing and debated aspects of Marxist thought down a rabbit hole, in this course we'll talk about this view as the **Process Narrative.**

In the Process Narrative of history, the conditions of life are constantly in flux, changing according to larger processes (forces) which conflict with each other. Value judgments about the past and the present are useless in this narrative, and a great example of how this plays out is to imagine an oak tree.

In the ProGress Narrative of history, the acorn from which the oak sprouted, or the sapling it became, are both lesser than the full-grown oak in the present.

In the ProCess Narrative, however, both the acorn and the oak are both processes of the same thing—in fact, the tree itself is a process, a thing always becoming, rather than a thing ever finished.

PROGRESS NARRATIVE
The idea that human society is constantly getting better, becoming more advanced and more free. In this view, the past was "backwards" and "dark" while the future will inevitably be even better than the present.

PROCESS NARRATIVE
A way of looking at the world and everything in it as things always in states of continual change and cycles. In this view, old and young, modern and primitive, and future and past are merely states of being, not value judgments.

If this way of looking at the world sounds a bit Pagan, it's because it is also an animist view, while the Progress Narrative is a Christian (primarily Protestant) view. Protestants tend to see the world as a progression from the fall of man in the Garden of Eden to the second coming of Jesus Christ (at which point history will be fulfilled). Animist cultures, on the other hand, tend to think more in mythic cycles or in non-linear time: stories, rather than histories.

Nature Is All

Marxist Historical Materialism (the Process Narrative) makes one other assertion that we'll need to understand before looking at the birth of capitalism.

That assertion is this: human thought reflects the material world because humans are part of that world. That is, there is no realm of "ideals" that exists before the world; everything that we think is a reflection of our experiences as humans living in societies that humans have created. The human body is not just something we live in but something that we are, and it's that experience of being human in the world which leads us to "discover" (really—to imagine) ideal situations.

Compare this to one of the foundational ideas of the Progress Narrative: that there is an "ideal state" of existence towards which society is always reaching (and, in the more Christian variants, an "ideal state" from which we have fallen and need to return). In that view, what is ideal already exists in our heads and it's that ideal against which we should judge human experience.

There's a simpler way of understanding this, one many Pagans are very familiar with. In many magical conceptions of the world, there are four elements which comprise all of existence: air, fire, water, and earth. These elements are always intermixing to create the world: for instance, the human body is comprised of earth (its structure and material existence), water (our bodies are mostly water and are flexible), air (the oxygen we breathe and the carbon dioxide we create), and fire (the heat we create and take in, the transmutation of food into energy). All of these elements are physical (material) forces that are always in relationship with each other.

In Western society, however, we tend to think of a split between mind (or spirit) and matter, and the mind/spirit is greater than matter. "Positive thinking" is one of the ways this manifests—if you just imagine yourself happy or rich, you'll become happy or rich. Putting an optimistic spin on life, or visualizing world peace: these are other consequences of this worldview.

A Marxist framework points to the actually-existing circumstances that are causing poverty and war, and show how material conditions lead to such suffering. In this way, the Marxist framework can be said to be more Pagan. It tells us to look at the world around us, study it, understand how processes work together for or against certain ways of being, and says that it isn't our theories and positive thinking that changes the world, it's our actions.

This framework is also deeply animist. It allows us to see the past and the people who lived in it not as failed "primitive" states but as part of the same processes which exist now. Our ancestors are not faded memories but parts of our lives in the same way that a fallen tree continues to nourish the forest it was a part of. The dead live on, not just in our thoughts but literally in the very fabric of our material existence. We walk on streets and live in buildings built by people who no longer live—their work continues to shape our daily existence, whether we acknowledge them or not.

Life Before And Outside Capitalism

In the thought experiment at the beginning of this chapter, I asked you to imagine what life might have been like for a commoner 500 years ago. The answer to this question is also the answer to what life was like for commoners 1000

The Birth & History of Capitalism

years ago or 2000 years ago. It's also what life is like now for people living in the few non-capitalist cultures still in existence, or what it's like for people such as the Amish, and what life would be like today if you suddenly moved with about 40 other people to a small village without electricity and modern technological devices.

Part of your daily life would be spent working, just as it is now. There's a pretty good chance you'd spend much of that work-time farming, raising your own food and livestock to provide food for yourself and your family. But you wouldn't be farming alone—you'd be farming with others in your village, dividing the tasks up amongst each other according to who was good at what.

You wouldn't be farming all year, by the way...you can't in most of the world. Farming is a task-related kind of work, and these tasks are determined by the time of year and the cycle of growth. So, for instance, at the beginning of spring you'd be very busy breaking up the ground and planting seeds, but after that your tasks become watering and weeding until the plants are ready to harvest. At that point you're really, really busy again, putting everything into storehouses, grinding grain, sorting seeds to save for the next year, and doing other activities related to that harvest (including brewing beer and cider). And then, come winter, there's no farming for you to do at all.

There would be many daily tasks as well. Every morning someone in your family would have to let all the animals out that you keep in coops, barns, or on the first floor of your house to protect them from wolves and foxes. You'd cook, draw water, clean, repair things, build things, create things. You might go hunting with others in the village, and have many other tasks that related to your daily survival.

Sounds like a lot of work? It is. But was it more work than what you're doing now? The answer in many cases is no.

Sure, you probably work forty hours a week at a job, and a peasant might spend many more hours than that farming some weeks. So it probably seems like they were doing more work than you do now.

But think again about how much work you *actually* do in a day, and this time, instead of just including the hours spent at a job, think about all the other work you do. If you drive to work, include that. If you have kids you have to get ready for school each morning, include that time. Also include the amount of time you spend cooking and cleaning and shopping, doing all those other activities that are required for living. That's all work, too.

Now, imagine all the time you currently get off from work. Unless you're a school teacher, you probably don't have a three-month period every year where you don't have to go to your job, huh?

For a peasant though, winter was a time of rest, where none of the manual labor in the fields was even possible. For us, however, work is usually the same throughout the year, always the same required 8 (or more) hours each day, and often times even busier during winter, especially if you work in retail or shipping in the months leading up to Christmas.

There is one major difference between the work done by a peasant and the work done by us now. That's this: often, almost all of the work a peasant did was for themselves. They didn't "go to work" for someone, they just worked. **In most of the history of humanity, the vast majority of what a human produced (the products of their work) were theirs to use, and what they produced that they didn't need (their surplus labor) they exchanged with others for things they didn't produce themselves.**

That doesn't mean everything they produced was theirs. Often, some of it was taken from them through force. Feudal land owners, warlords, kings, and even religious leaders took some of that surplus in the form of taxation, tithes, rent, and outright theft.

That part hasn't changed between the past and the present—governments still tax our work. But believe it or not, the amount that a peasant got to keep was often a much higher percentage than what we get to keep from our work. (We'll look at that more in depth in a bit).

How To Get Rich Without Earning It

We've talked about what commoners were usually doing before capitalism—what about the rich? How did they get their wealth?

Throughout most of human history, the primary way for the rich to gain wealth quickly was to take it. War, conquest, slavery, pillaging—these were the ways you got wealth (and still are often enough). Riding into a village with soldiers, demanding tribute (taxes) in the form of grain, livestock, or other goods was a time-honored way of gaining wealth for those who didn't work for it themselves.

If you had enough soldiers, you might enslave the villagers, but keeping slaves isn't as easy at it seems. You have to watch them, beat them, and generally terrify them into submission, and this requires more than just a few soldiers. You would need a systematic way to keep them from running away or refusing to work or rising up against you, as well as having overseers (whom you have to pay) and more soldiers to defend you in the middle of the night from a slave revolt.

Sounds a bit...inefficient? It is, actually: **slavery is a difficult system to maintain.** Imagine yourself attempting to enslave someone (an uncomfortable and awful thought, I know!): how would you not only keep them from running away or killing you, but also force them to do work for you? Only empires (the Roman, the Greek, the British, the Spanish, the Portuguese, the American, etc.) are ever really capable of that scale of systematic oppression for very long.

So though slavery has existed everywhere many times, it has never become the primary way for the rich to gain wealth. And there are only so many times you can pillage the countryside before there is nothing left to pillage, so violent theft of wealth is also not a "sustainable" system for very long unless you had a massive army (which you also have to pay and feed).

Instead of slavery and armed theft, **the primary method of gaining wealth that the rich have used before capitalism was taxation**, yearly tributes of an amount enough to keep the lords rich but not so high that the peasants revolted. Because that's always the other risk the rich face in their hunger for wealth—at any point, the people they take it from might decide to rise up against them. A handful of armed soldiers is no match for a hundred villagers armed with pitchforks, spears, and burning torches.

"Class struggle" existed before Capitalism. Those who want to take wealth from others have always had to worry about those they take from rising up against them. And those who produce wealth have always had to worry about those with weapons and power taking what they produce away from them. This is the point Marx and Engels make in the opening line of the first section of *The Communist Manifesto*:

> *"The history of all heretofore existing societies has been the history of class struggle..."*

As I mentioned above, certain ways of taking wealth from others (like slavery) require larger systems to maintain them. By systems I don't mean what we talk about when we say "systems of white supremacy" or "patriarchy" (we'll talk about those next chapter!) Rather, I mean physical systems: people and physical resources to enact those means.

Slavery, for instance requires slavers (armed people who would conquer, kidnap and transport slaves), overseers (people who would make sure the slaves were doing the work they were enslaved to do), soldiers or police (to catch slaves when they run away or defend the slave owners when they try to revolt), and also physical resources to maintain the slaves themselves (a slave you don't feed won't do work). All of this required a lot of wealth in the first place, and a lot of wealth to maintain, and the "risk" for the slave-owners of losing that wealth from revolts meant that few could really "afford" to keep slaves.

So from the point of view of the ruling classes (the wealthy, the nobility, etc.), finding a way to get labor (and therefore more wealth) from people that didn't rely on such a risky and resource-heavy system was vital. Pillaging works, but only so often (and again—you need soldiers for this). So in Europe, they found another system: feudalism.

Feudalism

Feudalism was born out of the collapse of the Roman Empire in Europe, but it took several centuries to fully take root. When Rome fell, Europe didn't just disappear into a "dark ages" until the Renaissance. In fact, "the dark ages" is another creation of the so-called Enlightenment. The world was hardly dark just because an empire collapsed. If anything, life got a little better for the poor and definitely a lot better for people previously enslaved by the Romans.

One class of people did suffer from the fall of empire, however—the wealthy.

The Roman Empire had created vast networks of trade (including laying down thousands of miles of roads), as well as building up many towns into military fortresses connected by those trade routes. Through its imperial bureaucracy and system of patronage, it also created a class of people with massive amounts of wealth, much of it in the form of land granted them by the empire. When that empire collapsed, they no longer had the backing of imperial armies and had to hire their own.

FEUDALISM
The dominant political and economic system in Europe between the ninth and fifteenth centuries. In feudalism, rich landowners (lords) supported stronger landowners (including kings) in return for military protection. Feudal lords controlled the peasants on their land and extracted a third of everything they produced in taxes. Those peasants were not allowed to leave the land or to marry without permission from the lord.

CHAPTER THREE

So life for common people after the fall continued as it had before, except that the armed men who would occasionally ride into the village demanding grain and sheep weren't Roman soldiers any longer. They were local strongmen, sometimes chieftains of tribal nations, Viking raiders, or the hired thugs of former Roman nobility or their descendents. Meanwhile, local customs and beliefs were able to flourish again in many places without Roman soldiers forcing people to convert to Christianity or face death.

Feudalism arose from this environment as the small wealthy class tried to consolidate power again, aided by the Christian Church and its network of priests and bishops. Religion was useful in this process: it helped give those the Church supported an air of legitimacy to their claims, and in return the priests gained powerful help in converting (or reconverting) peasants.

What is feudalism, though? It's a hierarchical political relationship in which rulers swore loyalty to stronger rulers, who in turn promised to protect them from other strong rulers.

Feudalism became useful for the wealthy for a reason I've already hinted at throughout this discussion of history. Remember: soldiers cost money, and without soldiers you cannot exploit peasants easily. You need an army to force people to pay taxes or tribute, and if those soldiers are constantly busy making sure the peasants don't revolt, they won't be able to defend your land from invasion. The same is true in reverse: if you send your army out to fight another army, the people you've been exploiting are likely to rise up while they're gone.

The political arrangement of feudalism solved this problem for the rich. By agreeing to give a portion of their own wealth to a king, they received the protection of a larger army and could then focus on gaining wealth from the commoners. The king also gained claim to their land in these arrangements, a fact that comes into play later in the history of Europe, leading to the creation of large kingdoms and empires like the British and Spanish.

Life Under Feudalism

Under feudalism, life got harder for commoners again. As lord and king laid claim to land with armies, those who lived on that land found themselves suddenly claimed as well. Feudal lords began claiming portions of everything the peasants (or serfs) produced, as well as forcing them to work directly for the lord during certain periods of the year.

Our image of what life was like for a serf often looks like a short life of tragedy and back-breaking work. And in some cases, this is indeed what life as a producer within feudalism looked like. It's quite possible this is also how they themselves saw their lives, especially those who themselves (or whose grandparents) remembered what life was like before serfdom. But there are some surprising aspects to life as a serf that may shift your opinion slightly.

For instance, a serf was sometimes required to give their feudal lord up to 1/3rd of everything they produced. Sounds like a lot, until you compare it to how much taxes are for many workers in modern nations now (including sales tax). And this comparison isn't even the half of it, because governments are not the only ones who take a portion of human labor under capitalism.

In fact, most small businesses cap their payroll for employees at a third of their total budget. That means they are taking 2/3rds of what employees "make" for the owner and

THE ROLE OF CHRISTIANITY IN FEUDALISM

The Church had a very important role in maintaining feudalism. Priests in every village often acted as spies for the feudal lords and preached obedience. This is because the Church relied on funding from the lords for their churches and the Pope and Bishops relied on kings for their protection. The Church also needed help from the lords to collect tithes, to convert Pagans and to kill heretics.

giving them no more than a third back. And that's for small businesses: larger businesses and corporations spend much smaller percentages of their revenue paying their workers.

So, serfs actually got to keep much more of what they produced than we do. In addition, **the amount of time actually spent working was less than most people now** (taking into account winters). And the amount of time serfs were forced to work without compensation for the lords was often only a few days per year.

Before we idealize feudal life too much, it's vital to understand one thing that serfs could not do. They couldn't leave the land. They belonged to the lord; they were the lord's serfs, and leaving often meant death if you were caught. Also, the lord had a lot of control over certain parts of the serf's life: for example, in many cases couples had to ask permission of the lord to marry, and the lord could (and did) in return demand the "right" to have sex with the woman first.

Another Shake-Up in Europe

Feudalism started in the 9th century, grew stronger for the next few hundred years, and then collapsed in the 15th century.

Most capitalist histories tell the story of its end as a natural transition to a more efficient system. Even many Marxist historians gloss over this transition, writing this change as if capitalism had merely been waiting for a chance to evolve from the feudal system. But one very important Marxist feminist scholar, Silvia Federici, makes clear that an event we all know of had much more importance to this change than we generally realise.

That event? The Black Death.

In the middle of the 1300's, between 30% to 60% of Europe's population died. Though the plague killed indiscriminately, by sheer percentage of the population, it was the peasants who suffered the most. And while it's impossible to understand what that much death must have been like, there was an unlooked-for boon for the poor from this carnage: because there were fewer of them, they were in higher demand by the wealthy.

When workers are easy to come by, the rich get away with exploiting them more. When there are fewer workers available, the rich have to do more to attract or keep them.

Consider: if a lord needs 10 serfs to produce all the wealth he demands but has a hundred serfs at his disposal, if a few of them die it is no great loss to him. But if he needs ten and only has ten, he can't work them as hard any longer. In return, the serfs understand this too, and are more likely to make successful demands that the lord must agree to.

So as perverse as it may sound, the Black Death actually ushered in a short period of power and freedom for peasants. They could leave the feudal manors and not worry that the lord's soldiers would chase them down because most of those soldiers had died anyway. And if they stayed, they could be in better positions to negotiate their own terms with the lord.

Of course, this meant that the rich faced another problem. The old agreements no longer worked, peasant revolts became common occurrences (most of the largest ones occurred in the 14th, 15th, and 16th centuries), and free towns (full of people with no feudal lord) as well as communes full of heretics arose throughout Europe.

The rich couldn't force people to work their land any longer; they had to find other ways to get them to do so.

THE BLACK DEATH

The Bubonic Plague, a disese which spread initially through fleas carried by rats and then eventually through air, killed between 30% and 60% of Europe's population, primarily in densely-populated areas. The societal breakdown it caused ironically helped the poor greatly: survivors fled manors and founded free towns, Pagan rites flourished in many places, and wages increased as the rich had a harder time finding workers.

CHAPTER THREE

Primitive Accumulation: Slavery & Colonization

Before we talk about the birth of capitalism from the ruins of feudalism, there's another process that we haven't spoken of yet and its of vital importance. That process is colonization.

Earlier in this chapter I explained how directly taking wealth from people is not a very sustainable system. Besides the initial cost of an army to conquer people with, communities can only be pillaged once or twice before there's nothing to take. You can ride into a village, kill all the men and steal all the gold in the houses only once before there's no more men to kill and no more gold to steal.

What was possible to pillage in Europe had mostly already been pillaged, especially as feudal holdings fell into ruin from lack of workers. Fortunately for the wealthy of Europe and unfortunately for the rest of the world, sea routes to the Americas were established.

COLONIZATION
Colonization is the conquest and settlement of foreign lands by a political power in order to extract wealth. Colonization isn't just settlement (migrants and refugees settle in new lands all the time).
Instead, colonies are set up for the sole purpose of expanding political and economic power.

Soon, ships full of soldiers arrived on the shores of both continents and "discovered" new villages to pillage, hauling gold, silver, furs, new foods, and slaves back to the coffers of king and merchant in Europe. The same happened in Africa and Asia: European lords competed with each other to pillage as much as possible in order to make up for the wealth they lost from the collapse of feudalism.

Slavery—which had almost completely ended in Europe after the fall of the Roman Empire—began again, but this time with slaves from Africa and the Americas.

There are several things to keep in mind when we look at how and why slavery began again during this period.

• First of all, like pillaging, **slavery is not a very sustainable system to maintain unless you have a lot of resources to**

begin with. In this case, unfortunately, that wasn't a problem: all the stolen wealth from the Americas was more than enough to hire soldiers, slavers, and overseers for this.

• Secondly: **slavery is a form of labor.** We tend to forget this when we think about slavery because the brutality of the system looms larger than the motives behind it. To gain wealth, you need humans to apply their labor to things. Slavery is a way of getting that labor, and though the circumstances of a slave are absolutely worse than the circumstances of a serf or worker, the reason for that exploitation is the same in all cases: the rich want more wealth.

• Third: The tactics used in the exploitation of slaves from Africa and the Americas were not invented when this period of colonial slavery began. Recall the conditions of a serf under feudalism, particularly in the control that a feudal lord exerted over the sexual life and mobility of the serfs. **Methods of control learned through the exploitation of peasants in Europe were applied in the institution of slavery.**

• Fourth: Slavery has occurred in many times and many places throughout the world, including both in Europe and also in many of the groups who were enslaved. **It also still occurs throughout the world.** This is a very tricky concept to discuss, since some groups insist that only chattel slavery (the sort of slavery that was forced upon African peoples) is "actual" slavery. In chattel slavery, the slave is fully-owned by the owner and is their "property." Oftentimes, this ownership of the slave also extends to their children as well.

CHATTEL SLAVERY
The most severe form of slavery, in which the slave and their offspring are fully owned by the slave-owner. The transatlantic slave trade that brought African slaves to the Americas was chattel slavery. The word chattel comes from the same Latin word from which we have both the words cattle and capital.

It's important to understand this distinction, but also to consider that other forms of slavery also exist too: for instance, women trafficked for unpaid sex-work, immigrant workers who are forced to work for free under threat of imprisonment, indentured servanthood as still practiced in the caste system of India or as occurred to Irish emigrants, and prison labor, especially amongst Black and other minority prisoners in the US. **These are all forms of slavery that vary in degrees of exploitation, and chattel slavery is undoubtedly the most severe of these forms.**

The use of slaves allowed the wealthy in Europe to circumvent the labor crisis they were facing in their own lands. Peasants in Europe had gained too much power to be easily exploited, so slavery was a means for the rich to continue extracting the labor of workers without ceding even more power to them.

PRIMITIVE ACCUMULATION
The process of gaining wealth (often violently) in order to later use that wealth as capital. Slavery, colonialism, pillaging, and Enclosure are all forms of primitive accumulation. The word primitive in this case means "primary" or "initial," and doesn't have the negative connotation the capitalist Progress Narrative gives it.

Not only that, but it then gave them access to the wealth they needed to fight back against the peasant revolts in Europe, as well as allowing even lesser lords a chance to usurp the hierarchy instituted by feudalism and become rulers in their own right.

It's absolutely essential to see this connection. The wealth stolen during colonization and the exploitation of labor through slavery didn't merely get stored in treasure chests within the throne rooms of kings and queens: it was used to gain more wealth, invested in new ways of extracting wealth from people and resources.

In Marxist terms, the period of extraction of wealth through plunder and slavery is called **Primitive Accumulation** (primitive means "first" or "initial" in this instance, not "backwards" or "savage" as we've come to understand it in the present). And all that wealth gained through primitive accumulation is what became the capital which now rules the world.

The Birth of Capitalism: Enclosure and Industrialisation

Remember how I mentioned that slavery requires people working in specific professions (slave-catcher, overseer, etc.) in order be sustainable? Imperialism does too, and more so. Merchants, book-keepers, appraisers, colonial administrators, bankers, and countless other "managerial" occupations are needed to keep an empire running.

The period of imperialist expansion saw an explosion of such professions, creating a new class of people above the workers but below the aristocrats. They lived mostly in towns and cities, partook in a greater share of the wealth coming from colonization than the workers, and also gravitated more towards the new "urban" Christianity (Protestantism) than the poor or the nobles did.

This class of people, the "bourgeoisie" (town-dwellers) began to exert a stronger influence on society than either of the two other groups. They tended to see themselves as the real power behind all the new wealth circulating throughout Europe (and to some degree they were right—they were the managers—though not the creators—of all this wealth).

They also saw themselves as more educated and creative than the ruling class (who were both very traditional and also very cautious with their wealth), and often times more "moral." This last part comes from the sort of Protestant Christianity they favored most: Calvinism, which taught that wealth, self-discipline, and strict public morality were signs of God's favor, that they were part of the "elect" whom God had chosen for salvation.

Calvinism is crucial to understanding how Capitalism developed, as it had even more of an influence than Lutheranism or

CALVINISM

A Protestant version of Christianity founded by John Calvin. It teaches that God has predestined his chosen people and that wealth is a sign of God's favor. It also taught that hard work and a strict morality made you holy. The Puritans who colonized New England were Calvinists.

Catholicism. Calvinism represented several significant breaks in worldview from the Catholic worldview, not least of which was its end to the prohibition against usury (lending money with interest).

Catholicism, while not at all a religion particularly kind to the poor, nevertheless maintained certain limits on the way the poor could be treated. Within Catholicism it would be sinful to charge so much for food that the poor would starve, for instance. Calvinism rejected such an idea and instead even suggested it was the duty of merchants to inflate prices so as to keep the poor from being lazy or overfed.

Also, **Calvinism viewed the natural world as something God made for his chosen people to use; thus, a forest only had value as something to be used, not as something in-itself.**

So, we have a new group of people, armed with a new religious view, quickly gaining more wealth and political power in Europe. And we have an aristocracy (still recovery from the collapse of the feudal system) utterly reliant on this class of people.

And what about the poor? Life for them got even harder. As this new class of people (the bourgeoisie) arose, they began to demand more land from governments, in particular from the parliament in England. They (and especially one of their philosophers, Adam Smith), argued that unproductive land was useless and possibly sinful, and English parliament gave them what they wanted in the form of several waves of En-closure Acts.

These laws subdivided large plots of land (literally enclos-ing them in fences or hedges) which were then sold by the government. The "unproductive land" they targeted for these enclosures and sales didn't come from the aristocrats, how-ever, it came from the poor.

Under feudalism, serfs were given access to shared plots of land they could use for their own needs. Small woodlands were full of animals that could be hunted for food and leather as well as wood for building and heating; meadows and grasslands could be used for grazing sheep and cattle as well as growing food, and streams and ponds were sources of water and fish for the peasants.

Right to use this land had been enshrined in common law for centuries, concessions won by people as early as the beginning of feudalism. A cognate of this sort of land might be the small garden plots plantation owners allowed slaves to cultivate for their own food; though it was officially not the property of the slaves, it was land the owner set aside for their use and knew that, if he were to take it away from them, they would likely starve or revolt.

THE COMMONS
Land and other resources that were shared amongst a community for their collective use. For instance, rivers for fishing, water, and bathing; forests for hunting, wood, and foraging; and meadows for grazing, growing food, and community events.

It was this very land, "the Commons," that the English parliament and large landholders enclosed and then sold off. Each meadow fenced off, each woodland cut down, and each stream and pond blocked off meant many hungry peasants suddenly with no means to survive. There were revolts against these actions, oftentimes led by women, and always put down violently by militia, landowners, and soldiers.

Enclosure spread quickly from England to Scotland and Ireland, then to France and what is now Germany, and soon Europe saw the greatest displacement it had ever seen. Peasants and small farmers suddenly had no land to live on: their only option was to move to the towns and cities to find work or become part of the settlements in the colonized lands. Most went to the towns, but when they got there, they found them already overflowing with other displaced peasants also looking for work.

ENCLOSURE
The act of turning public land and other resources into private property.

like a feudal lord, he forbade his workers to leave the town where the factory was located.

It took very little time for this new way of using the labor of workers to spread throughout Europe. Factories sprung up quickly in the American colonies, primarily those (like Richard Arkwright's first factory) devoted to turning the cotton picked by African slaves into cloth and clothing to then be sold in the cities crowded with displaced people working in similar factories elsewhere.

INDUSTRIALIZATION
A way of organizing and exploiting labor in which work is done in factories, mills, and other large-scale situations. In industrial capitalism, workers are treated like machines with only a few tasks they must repeat for hours on end.

This is a vital point—**the labor exploited through slavery and the labor exploited in factories is connected**, and not just because they were both forms of exploited labor. They were applying labor to the very same resources, just at different parts of the chain.

Just as now in Africa a child mines coltan that is then used in manufacturing of smartphones by poorly-paid factory workers in China, the exploitation of slave labor and factory labor was put in place by the same forces and by same people, stringing together the suffering of one group with the suffering of another in order gain more wealth.

This is the chain of suffering that Marx saw, writing less than a century after the first factory arose in England. The vampiric nature of capital, "dead labor" (and include in that dead slaves!) that "sucks the life of living labor."

The bourgeoisie—this new managerial class—had learned how to harness the power of workers in a way the feudal lords had never been able to achieve. Not just the power of their own workers, but those elsewhere, people colonized and enslaved across an ocean. A new system had arisen, one which now seems to have no end.

Study Questions & Further Reading

1. The Progress Narrative is one of the hardest aspects of modern capitalist society to confront, as it affects not only how we see the past but also how we see the present. The idea that things are "always getting better" can be seen everywhere: from human rights and social justice to tech gadgets and automobiles. Yet Climate Change, mass extinction events, and increasing poverty are never included in this idea. In the next few days, look for examples of how the Progress Narrative seems to be fed to us, especially through media. Also, when you imagined a medieval peasant, how much of this picture was constructed from images you've seen on film or television?

2. The Process Narrative doesn't make value judgments between the past and the present, but rather sees history as a constant "unfolding" or "becoming." When you think of your own life, how might this narrative change the way you think about age, guilt, and intelligence? And how might is also change the way you think about political events around you?

3. Modern life is saturated with machines, devices, and technologies that claim to make life "easier" for us, and this is one of the reasons we tend to imagine life in the past as more difficult than the present. But with each time-saving machine often comes the imperative to use it. If you drive a car, how does the distance you "can" travel to work become the distance you "must" travel to work? If you have a smart phone, do you find yourself constantly working even when not at work? In what other ways might modern technology not represent a net decrease to the amount of work a peasant might have done?

4. Defining slavery as any form of co-erced, uncompensated labor is not without controversy. Consider researching at least one incident of modern slavery. How does the "form" of slavery persist across time even as the specific conditions change?

5. The Commons in Europe functioned very similar to the way that many indigenous peoples in North America used and shared land, so much so that many Anarchists and communists in the 19th century studied the way First Nations used land as a way of reclaiming the Commons in Europe. What parallels can be drawn from the Enclosure of the Commons in Europe and the theft of land from colonized peoples? What are the differences?

6. Take an item of clothing or technology in your home and try to trace where every aspect of it came from. Then try to draw a line of production between the raw resources and you as the final consumer. What are the conditions of workers along that line? How are you connected to them?

Further Reading

Light:
On peasant vacation time: https://nypost.com/2013/09/04/medieval-peasants-got-a-lot-more-vacation-time-than-you-economist/

Moderate:
The Revolutionary Dead: Karl Marx part 2
https://abeautifulresistance.org/site/2015/11/13/the-revolutionary-dead-karl-marx-part-2
A New Luddite Rebellion:
https://abeautifulresistance.org/site/2018/02/14/a-new-luddite-rebellion

Intensive:
Time, Work-Discipline, and Industrial Capitalism: an essay by historian EP Thompson on how the modern conception of time was inculcated into workers. http://www.sv.uio.no/sai/english/research/projects/anthro-pos-and-the-material/Intranet/economic-practices/reading-group/texts/thompson-time-work-discipline-and-industrial-capital-ism.pdf

CHAPTER FOUR:
The Social Costs
of Capitalism

We've examined how political and economic life changed, but we have yet to look at how the social existence of people was transformed by capitalism. To understand this, we'll look deeper into what Marx has to say about social conditions in The Communist Manifesto.

The Social Management of the World

In *The Communist Manifesto*, Marx and Engels focus heavily on the influence of the bourgeoisie and their political and social power. Understanding the rise of the bourgeois ethic is essential to understanding how our social relations are determined by capitalism. To understand this, let's look at one particular section of *The Communist Manifesto*, the part where the bourgeosie are described. Don't worry if you don't immediately understand everything here–we'll go into each of those sections in depth.

> *The bourgeoisie, wherever it has got the upper hand, has put an end to all feudal, patriarchal, idyllic relations. It has pitilessly torn asunder the motley feudal ties that bound man to his "natural superiors", and has left remaining no other nexus between man and man than naked self-interest, than callous "cash payment". It has drowned the most heavenly ecstasies of religious*

fervour, of chivalrous enthusiasm, of philistine sentimentalism, in the icy water of egotistical calculation. It has resolved personal worth into exchange value, and in place of the numberless indefeasible chartered freedoms, has set up that single, unconscionable freedom — Free Trade. In one word, for exploitation, veiled by religious and political illusions, it has substituted naked, shameless, direct, brutal exploitation.

The bourgeoisie has stripped of its halo every occupation hitherto honoured and looked up to with reverent awe. It has converted the physician, the lawyer, the priest, the poet, the man of science, into its paid wage labourers.

The bourgeoisie has torn away from the family its sentimental veil, and has reduced the family relation to a mere money relation.

The bourgeoisie has disclosed how it came to pass that the brutal display of vigour in the Middle Ages, which reactionaries so much admire, found its fitting complement in the most slothful indolence. It has been the first to show what man's activity can bring about. It has accomplished wonders far surpassing Egyptian pyramids, Roman aqueducts, and Gothic cathedrals; it has conducted expeditions that put in the shade all former Exoduses of nations and crusades.

The bourgeoisie cannot exist without constantly revolutionising the instruments of production, and thereby the relations of production, and with them the whole relations of society. Conservation of the old modes of production in unaltered form, was, on the contrary, the first condition of existence for all earlier industrial classes. Constant revolutionising of production, uninterrupted disturbance of all social conditions, everlasting uncertainty and agitation distinguish the bourgeois epoch from all earlier ones. All fixed, fast-frozen relations, with their train of ancient and venerable prejudices and opinions, are swept away, all new-formed ones become antiquated before they can ossify. All that is solid melts into air, all that is holy is profaned, and man is at last compelled to face with sober senses his real conditions of life, and his relations with his kind.

The end of Feudal social relations

(How the new capitalist class changed the general social fabric of societies)

> *"The bourgeoisie, wherever it has got the upper hand, has put an end to all feudal, patriarchal, idyllic relations. It has pitilessly torn asunder the motley feudal ties that bound man to his "natural superiors", and has left remaining no other nexus between man and man than naked self-interest, than callous "cash payment".*

We've already seen that feudalism was an exploitative system, but under feudalism, lords were were not able to fully exploit their serfs. In fact, feudal lords often needed to make concessions to their serfs, needed to protect them from other lords, give them access to common land, and obey many other informal (and sometimes written) customs as part of *noblesse oblige* (noble obligations).

These were not moral duties the feudal lords merely volunteered to do as part of their responsibility as nobles, however: instead, many parts of these codes were concessions the lords were forced to make in order to stop peasant strikes or revolts.

CHAPTER FOUR

The idea that rulers must act justly and be held to higher standards of moral behavior because of their position continues to this day. Think about the corruption scandals surrounding presidents and prime ministers constantly filling newspapers and the media. When a president has sex with an intern or a prime minister uses their position to gain wealth, we judge them more harshly than when a CEO does the same thing, precisely because of this older moral code.

Why do we exempt the CEO? It isn't because they have less political power than a politician (compare the political power of a US representative or UK member of parliament to the power of a CEO of Goldman Sachs, Nestle, or Exxon!) Instead, it's because the bourgeoisie, in usurping the economic power of the feudal lords, managed to exempt themselves from the old order of obligations.

Charles Dickens' famous story, *A Christmas Carol*, written during the period of this transition, illustrates this shift very well. The refusal of Ebeneezer Scrooge, the uncaring boss, to give his worker any extra money during Christmas seems bad enough to us now. It is even worse when we consider that giving serfs and commoners cake, brandy, and time off from work during Christmas was considered part of the duty of feudal lords under *noblesse oblige* for centuries.

In fact, many modern Christmas traditions still echo this older feudal order. Caroling itself was part of this system: peasants and townsfolk sang raucous songs outside the homes of the wealthy lords demanding food and alcohol. If the lords did not oblige, the carolers would break in and take what they wanted. That's why Dickens' story is named *A*

> **NOBLESSE OBLIGE**
> The informal systems of rights and obligations of the rich under feudalism. Lords were bound to protect the serfs on their land, but also claimed certain rights (like the right to have sex with a serf on their wedding night). This system was upheld by custom, religion, and sometimes (in the case of obligations to serfs) by riot and violence from peasants.

Christmas Carol: it is an ironic play upon the older social relations, and those who read it when it came out would have understood his point.

That point? That the new order of bosses and owners was failing to fulfill its social obligations to those it exploited.

Both Dickens and Marx saw the same thing: **while the old order of feudalism was corrupt and oppressive, this new bourgeois/capitalist order was even more oppressive because it abolished all the rights earned by serfs**.

While feudal lords often tried hard to shirk their obligations to the peasants, the capitalist acknowledged no obligation or duty to his workers. Workers needed to provide everything for themselves now, and the only means by which they could do this (because there were no longer any Commons) was by working for the capitalist. That's the "cash payment" referred to in this section: the wage.

PAGAN CUSTOMS & PEASANT REVOLTS

Many holy days in Europe were survivals from pre-Christian Pagan festivals and customs which the Catholic Church re-named and repurposed. Later attempts by Protestant capitalists to end these customs were often met with violent revolt. One such sacred day, Beltane (1 May) continues and is now celebrated internationally as a day of worker revolts

The Change in Family Relations

How the capitalist class created a systematic subjugation of women.

> *"The bourgeoisie has torn away from the family its sentimental veil, and has reduced the family relation to a mere money relation."*

It is often difficult for us to conceive of this, but **the nuclear family, with its dominant husband and dutiful housewife, is a very new creation. More so, it's a capitalist creation.**

Just as it is incorrect to see history as a march of progress for the poor, it is also incorrect to see capitalism as part of a narrative of progress and liberation for women. In the feudal period and prior to that, as well as in countless societies outside Europe, women often had rights to property and access to more wealth than they did during the birth of capitalism.

The key to understanding how the position of women got worse under capitalism is the end of the Commons. When women and men both had access to meadows, streams, and woodlands they also had access to their own means of production. And while both had relatively equal access to the Commons before Enclosure, it was women who benefited most from this access.

Consider: unless there are social programs, a single woman with a child under capitalism has two primary means of survival: work for a wage or get married to a man who works for a wage. If she chooses the latter, the man will likely expect her to do domestic work (cook, clean, go shopping, raise children) in return for his financial support. He is able to offer this because of his wage, the money he earns from selling his labor to a capitalist. She on the other hand usually cannot make the same offer back to him: it's rare for a woman within capitalist societies to earn the same amount as a man might for similar work. Also, if she decides to sell her labor to a capitalist directly (for a wage) instead of getting married, she has to work more because of the child she is also supporting.

In feudal, tribal, and other societies outside capitalism, such a woman had another option—raise food for herself and her child without selling her labor to anyone. Along with this option she also had benefit

WOMEN & ENCLOSURE

When the Commons were sold off as private property, women suffered most and became more dependent upon men. So it's not suprising that many of the riots that occurred during this time were led by women. These actions often involved tearing down newly-built fences and hedgerows, as well as attacking and poisoning the new landlords.

of communal social relations in which women shared the work of child care, domestic labor (cooking meals, for instance), and also food production (raising crops, tending livestock).

Because of her access to land, her decision to enter a domestic relationship with a man was not often an imperative for survival, and if the man demanded too much labor from her, leaving him did not mean losing the ability to eat.

This order of things was destroyed by the Enclosures both in Europe and the colonized lands. Suddenly women found themselves with no choice but to either get married or work for someone else. Getting married, though, also meant working for someone else, especially because most capitalists favored male workers instead of female ones.

The reasons for this preference is not just that capitalists were often men themselves and adopted the patriarchal morality of Calvinism, though both are important factors. Another logic came into play for the owners: women gave birth to children, and pregnancy, child-birth, and taking care of an infant (breastfeeding, etc) got in the way of the capitalist's need for reliable, efficient workers.

So capitalists favored male workers, paying them higher wages than women. This division further entrenched the inequality women suffered because of the end of the Commons, and solidified a new form of family (the "nuclear" family) and a new division of labor, the housewife.

The Management of Society

How the capitalist class created a new "work morality" within society.

> *"The bourgeoisie cannot exist without constantly revolutionising the instruments of production, and thereby the relations of production, and with them the whole relations of society."*

As I noted in the last chapter, it's important to remember that the bourgeoisie was a managerial class. They studied how to increase the efficiency of workers, using new scientific methods developed by people whose livelihood came from the capitalists who paid them for their discoveries. Machines that required fewer workers to produce more goods, innovations such as steam and later combustion and electricity, and then assembly lines and automation have all been the legacy of this research.

The managerial logic of the capitalists is not just relevant to their ability to manage factories and other industries, but how to manage workers themselves.

Beginning in the 19th century, hundreds of moral primers were written to teach the poor how to be better workers, how to become more self-disciplined and thrifty with their wages, how to act civil in public, and how to avoid such sins as drinking (which makes workers late for work the next day). It will probably come as no surprise that these primers—and the many sermons preached by Protestant moralists—also included instructions on how women were to submit to their husbands and raise their children, and directions for husbands on how to manage their wives.

Calvinism became the perfect ideology for the transformation of displaced poor people into efficient cogs in the capitalist machine. But like everything else they touched, the bourgeoisie transformed Calvinism itself into something that could be exported into non-Calvinist societies. This ideology is often called the "mechanistic worldview," because its primary metaphor was the machine. Clocks, particularly, became the main image by which people began to describe the order of the

THE MECHANISTIC WORLDVIEW
The moral, intellectual, and ideological framework that arose with the birth of capitalism. In this worldview, the machine became the primary metaphor for life, nature, work, society, and even God. This worldview continues in the way we talk about ourselves as machines and computers (for instance, "having a breakdown" or "I need time to process that."

universe. Deism, the theology of many of the "founding fathers" of the United States, saw God as a "clockmaker" who had wound the universe up and set it in motion.

In such a worldview, "men of science" saw their role as merely discovering the rules God had set in place for the operation of humanity. The legacy of this worldview stays with us: modern medicine, genetics, biology, and even social sciences like psychology and history are all founded upon the idea that there are natural laws which determine human interactions and development. Race theory and eugenics are both also legacies of this worldview.

The end result of all this research, of schooling (compulsory education started during this time), and of an explosion of new laws against uncivilized behavior was to educate and punish out human behaviours that did not benefit the new capitalist order. Waking early, being "industrious," courteous to bosses, not loud or unruly in public spaces, and being punctual were just some of the values which arose during this period, each of which helped create a more disciplined working class.

This "management" of human behaviour extended also to the study of human movement and efficiency, giving rise to a systematic prejudice against people who were not able to be optimal workers. **Much of our current societal disgust of or prejudice against disabled people, for instance, can be traced to the capitalists' obsession with the bodies of workers**: what made them good cogs, what made them inefficient ones.

Managing the Division of Labor: Gender

A topic that deserves a book of its own is the way that the new capitalist class legislated divisions between the lower classes according to race, gender, and other identities.

We've looked a little at this already with the "management of the family," in which moralist preachers and writers advised women on how to manage their households and submit to their husbands. The results of these moral lessons were to create familial pressure on women (from their husbands and also from their children) to labor for them, but the pressure was even greater on the level of society.

Women who didn't care for their families, didn't keep clean homes and care for their exhausted husbands became seen as morally bankrupt and worthy of shame. Single women became seen as dangerous to society and potential saboteurs of communities.

In the period before the beginning of capitalism, independent women were typically accused of witchcraft. As the mechanistic worldview replaced the older worldviews, women continued to be suspect, but instead of being seen as witches they were often diagnosed with hysteria or other new medical conditions.

While women who did not submit to the dominant order in the feudal period and the transition to capitalism were often burned at the stake, under capitalism they were hospitalized against their wills and subjected to medical experiments and "treatments" which might have made The Inquisition proud. Electroshock, removal of the uterus or other female reproductive organs, treatments with new "medicines" now used in chemical warfare, and even lobotomies: these were all employed to manage women who did not fit into bourgeois norms.

Even women who did not undergo any of these "treatments" learned the required lesson, just as a public whipping of a slave serves as a threat to all the other slaves what will happen if they fail to perform their duties.

> **DIVISION OF LABOR**
> The way that work is assigned to people according to race, class, gender, and physical or intangible characteristics For instance, women are assigned emotional and domestic labor more often than men, immigrants are assigned more agricultural labor, poor males more factory and manual labor.

Dividing The Lower Classes

Before we talk about the way the capitalists managed the conquered peoples, many of them slaves, **we need to discuss the role men played in the subjugation of women.** You may have been wondering: where were the husbands, brothers, sons, friends, and fathers of those women who were subjected to those treatments? In fact, we can ask the same question about men during the witch hunts—as historians have shown, very, very few men ever intervened to stop this violence.

A common answer to this question is "the patriarchy," and that men have "always" subjugated women.

This is an insufficient answer, though, because while it seems to explain this problem in a neat and clean matter, it doesn't explain what is actually happening. Reducing this matter to a principle like this also follows too close to the Mechanistic Worldview, in which there are inherent laws of nature that determine human behavior (in this case, it's in the physical or social "nature" of men to subjugate women).

PATRIARCHY
A system in which men are given preferential treatement over women. Capitalism is a patriarchal system.

For a better answer, we need to try to see the world from the viewpoint of the ruling classes and their need to exploit labor to gain wealth. And we can see this best when we look at a common practice in corporate offices and businesses now.

Bosses often offer to certain workers higher wages or more benefits than to others according to their perceived loyalty. Usually, those workers will be told that they are getting paid more than another worker and will be asked not to disclose their pay to anyone.

This extra benefit is a managerial tactic, and an incredibly useful one if your goal is to reward loyalty and isolate disloyal employees. The person receiving the benefit might think it is very unfair that they are getting paid more than others, but they also probably need the extra money. They're quite likely to keep silent about the raise and feel an extra loyalty to their boss rather than their co-workers. They might even confide in the boss, report a co-worker who is stealing or not doing as much work as they're being paid for. And they will probably also keep silent when a co-worker is fired unjustly.

This tactic isn't new. It's been used by rulers for thousands of years. Roman slave-owners would grant some slaves more freedom than others in return for their help keeping the other slaves in line. Feudal lords would grant some serfs more access to the manor and reduce their tribute in exchange for reporting on serfs who were stealing from the lord. And on plantations in the United States, "house slaves" were also given more freedom and better food than the "field slaves" in order to gain their loyalty.

In every one of these examples, it's easy to see why a certain part of the lower classes might accept this devil's bargain. Getting better living conditions (higher pay, fewer beatings) for yourself is an obviously good thing. When those better conditions come at the expense of others, moral fortitude alone is often not enough to prevent a person accepting such a deal. It is only when you already have a strong loyalty (through love, community, etc.) to those who will be harmed by your acceptance of such a bargain that refusal becomes an easy matter.

Dividing the loyalty of workers is an essential management skill for a capitalist, just as it was for the feudal lords and slave-owners, as well as for the rulers of towns and bishops of the Church. Giving one group access to more freedom and wealth than another group is the best way to do this, especially when you construct a moral order that solidifies the differences between those groups.

In Catholicism and Calvinism both, women were seen as weaker and morally-fragile, witches or hysterics or temptresses who could not but help undermine the lives of men.

The Social Costs of Capitalism

Granting men the freedom from being burned at the stake in exchange for their silence worked, just as granting men higher pay and more access to wealth in our modern period also works.

Managing the Division of Labor: Race

With this in mind, we can now look at the construction of race.

It's first of all an incredibly difficult truth to hold that race as a category of human is a very new idea. There were no "white" people and "black" people in the middle ages of Europe (or anywhere else for that matter), nor was there any framework for seeing such a division of peoples except for religion.

The roots of the capitalist conception of race are found in a Catholic doctrine which saw all baptised peoples as part of one "communion" and all others as outside that communion. If you were within this communion, you were protected by the moral laws of the Church. Murder or enslavement of another Christian were "sins" that could result in excommunication, but this punishment did not extend to the same acts against unbaptized peoples in the rest of the world.

Thus, the Crusades were "moral" because they were slaughters enacted upon unbelievers outside of this communion, and the same was true for the slaughters enacted by Christian colonizers in Africa, Asia, and the Americas.

A difficult truth that this points to is that slavery and the murder of indigenous peoples wasn't done under the framework of race. Race didn't exist yet: the moral justifications for these horrors were that the peoples who suffered were not Christian.

RACE

A way of dividing humans that arose with capitalism in which humans with certain characteristics (primarily skin color and geographical origin) are categorized differently than those with other characteristics or origins.

However, as the dominance of the Church began to fade, rulers and those involved in the management of the slave trades and colonies needed to find a new moral framework to continue this exploitation. Race served this need perfectly, and helped satisfy another need: to keep the people they exploited from uniting together against their bosses.

In the colonies of North America and the Caribbean, colonial administrators began to see large uprisings composed of enslaved Africans, indigenous people, and poor immigrants from Europe. Many of those immigrants, remember, had only recently been forced off their own lands in England, Scotland, Wales, and Ireland during the Enclosures and had little loyalty to the colonial administrators (many of whom had also administered the Enclosures!)

Though their conditions were somewhat better than the slaves in the colonies, they had more in common with the slaves than with the people who ruled over them. They had sex with each other, learned from each other, and often left the colonies together, creating communities that threatened the stability of the wealth-extraction that the colonies represented.

The very first legal introduction of race occurred in the North American colonies in the 17th century. Laws were passed which forbade the intermixing of European immigrants with the conquered indigenous peoples and the enslaved Africans, as well as any transfer of wealth to these latter groups.

Rather than use the word "Christian" or "European" to define those who were granted more rights, the colonial administrators used the word "white," defining them by their skin color rather than their religion.

The use of the word "white" had several implications.

• First of all, it presented a very easy way for rulers to determine who was "in" and who was "out," especially since many Africans and indigenous peoples either converted to Christianity or mixed Christianity with their Pagan beliefs.

The Social Costs of Capitalism

• Secondly, it created a new framework of division between the lower classes that had not existed before: though certainly the conditions of immigrants from Europe and slaves from Africa were different from each other, there was no sense that it was because of their skin color that these conditions were different.

• And most crucial for the rulers, **"white" helped the rich obscure their own exploitation of the poor by creating an identity to which both the rulers and one group of the poor shared,** an identity which set them in opposition together against the darker-skinned slaves and natives.

As a tool of management, race spread very quickly throughout the colonies and back to Europe, where the "men of science" set about "discovering" the "natural differences" between the races. Measuring skulls and other parts of the body (whether the victim was dead or alive didn't matter), experimenting on darker-skinned peoples and even torturing them resulted in new categories of racial difference: Mongoloids, Causcasians, Negros, and then later many others, all accompanied by esoteric theories on their origins, limits, and capacity for learning, obedience, and labor.

The Nazi classifications of people into races and the awful experiments they put them through before killing them in the concentration camps were a legacy of this process begun centuries before. So, too, the theories of eugenicists and present-day scientists who claim to find inherent weaknesses and strengths in racial groups are continuations of capitalist racial management theories.

As with the silence and complicity of men in the face of torture and murder of women, those identified as "white" within capitalist societies likewise face (and too often accept) the devil's bargain of the capitalists.

Granting part of the lower classes more benefits ("privileges") on account of their skin color is the small price the capitalists pay for the silence and complicity of the "white" lower classes, as well as ensuring the lower classes do not unite together against them.

Race as a management tool has been terrifyingly effective. We need only look at the current situations in the United States to see its power: not only do poor whites and poor blacks rarely organize against the capitalists, but both groups often blame each other for the root of their suffering. In fact, capitalists heavily rely on racial hatred to undermine any threat to their power, and a brief glance at capitalist media (news programs, television, films) shows that they spend a lot of money maintaining this division. This media is not very different from the moral primers of the 18th and 19th centuries, propaganda to create exactly the sort of worker the capitalists require.

PRIVILEGE
A crucial part of capitalist management, privilege is any right or benefit given to one group of workers over another group. This can take many forms, but the important thing to remember is that privilege is a capitalist method of control, not an inherent trait.

The Society of the Market

How the capitalists brought all of human life under the imperative of the Market.

We come now to the final section of the quoted text from *The Communist Manifesto*, which contains the phrase after which this book is named.

> All fixed, fast-frozen relations, with their train of ancient and venerable prejudices and opinions, are swept away, all new-formed ones become antiquated before they can ossify. All that is solid melts into air, all that is sacred is profaned, and man is at last compelled to face with sober senses his real conditions of life, and his relations with his kind.

As we've seen, the management logic of the bourgeoisie was mechanistic and informed by Calvinist doctrines. While many (or likely most) of the current ruling capitalist classes of the world are unlikely to consider themselves Calvinist, this worldview is the dominant one in capitalist societies.

If anything, it is more accurate to say that the capitalist worldview was born from the Calvinist and mechanistic logic, but has become something which is now more dominant than both.

Ellen Meiksins Woods points out in her book, *The Origins of Capitalism: A Longer View,* that the greatest difference between capitalist societies and all the societies that existed before is the "market imperative." In capitalism, the market determines all other aspects of social life, so that we make our decisions and shape our existence around the demands of the market.

This is true in my own life as much as it likely is in yours. I moved to France last year because I could no longer afford to have the sort of life I wanted in America while doing the sort of work I wanted. I could not afford to be a writer and the managing editor of Gods&Radicals in Seattle, a city I dearly loved, because rents (determined by market forces) were too high, as were groceries (the market) and the cost of an afternoon at a cafe or a brief night out at a bar (again, market forces). And leaving Seattle for France required leaving many of my friends and loved ones, meaning that the market for rents and my own "job market" determined which people I could be around.

Not only are where I live and who I can be determined by the market, but the market imperative also determines what I do and

MARKET IMPERATIVE
Under capitalism, economic logic now dominates all other considerations. In pre-capitalist and non-capitalist societies, other considerations (religious, traditional, civil, moral, environmental, etc.) often trumped the demand for profit. In capitalism, one need only look at Climate Change to see how profit now dominates over all other concerns, even the future of earth itself.

create. This book? I've wanted to write this for years, but because I could not afford to spend the time to write without compensation, it's not until now that I finally could.

Note the word I used in that last sentence: *spend*. We "spend" and "save" and "buy" time; we "pay" attention. The logic of capital shapes the way we view our time on this earth so that we speak of it in terms of the market.

This occurs not just in English: in French, there is no easy or direct way to say that you "enjoyed" your experience with someone without economic language. One says "*J'ai profité des temps avec toi*" (I have profited from the time with you) or "*J'ai apprecié*" ("appreciated," which means "to assign increased value" just as a house appreciates in price).

Even who we choose to love is shaped by the capitalist market. How many relationship problems occur over money? How many relationships end or never start because of clashing economic status? And how much of what we choose to focus on in our lives is limited by whether or not we can "afford" to give those things our attention?

Just as our personal lives are shaped by the imperative of the market, so too is the way we view the rest of the world. Nature, particularly, suffers the most from this. Countless forests and entire species of plants, animals, and insects disappear from the face of the earth every year because the value those things had to the market was higher than the value we placed on their continued existence.

In non-capitalist societies, the natural world was not a thing to be bought and sold. Animist cultures saw the world full of spirit or spirits, persons with their own existence that could not be reduced to what price a human could get for it. A mountain could not be blown apart to get at the coal underneath because the mountain was a being of its own, sometimes a god, sometimes an ancestor, but never a thing to be made subservient to the economic activities of peoples.

The Social Costs of Capitalism

Even within Europe this view existed, persisting even into the feudal period and under the dominance of the Catholic Church. When Martin Luther and John Calvin railed against the Catholic Church during the 16th century, they condemned priests for still allowing peasants to believe the forests were full of spirits. Catholicism had tolerated Pagan beliefs to persist in Europe; the iconoclast riots (a movement of Calvinists who smashed statues of saints, overturned standing stones and demolished holy wells) were physical attempts to eradicate these older beliefs. But outside of Europe, especially in North and South America, both Catholic and Protestant missionaries and colonial administrators used forced education, the kidnapping of children, and torture to destroy these older worldviews.

> *"All that is sacred is profaned, all that is solid melts into air."*

This is the dark magic of capitalism, the esoteric power behind the imperative of the market and the exploitation of the world. Sweeping away all "fixed, fast-frozen relations" of humans with each other and of humans with the rest of the world, with their "train of ancient and venerable" opinions about what is truly valuable and what should not be destroyed. And we are left now to face "with sober senses" our real conditions of life and our real conditions with each other.

Study Questions &
Further Reading

1. We're often taught to see the end of feudalism as a net gain for humanity, but in many ways, it might be said that one awful system was replaced with another. How does the dominance of the current capitalist class differ from the dominance of those of feudal lords? How are they mere continuations of the same?

2. The loss of the Commons is seen not just by Marxist feminists as a direct crime on women. Indigenous women activists, especially in the Global South, see the continued capitalist Enclosures as a war on women's wisdom and power. How does this change or inform your view of feminism? And how does this relate to or conflict with "mainstream" feminism's focus on equality in the capitalist workplace?

3. Many behaviours we now consider decent, polite, or civil are a legacy of the Calvinist/capitalist push for morality. Deodorant and daily showers with soap, for instance, are only recent cultural "norms." If you consider yourself "middle class," how much of your perception of the hygeine or social behaviours of the poor might be part of this legacy? And what other social norms might this include?

4. The Marxist framework and the social justice framework both have very similar things to say about identity-based oppression, but often come to different conclusions about what to do about it. I present here the Marxist view—how does this compare to what you have elsewhere learned about social justice, privilege, racism, etc.? Do you find this framework less adequate, more adequate, or a mix of both?

5. The "disenchantment of the world" is something that Pagans actively fight. How does this disenchantment and the "mechanistic" view of the world relate?

The Social Costs of Capitalism

6. The reality that race is a very recent creation is difficult for us to comprehend, especially since, like capitalism, racism seems always to have existed. But the end of capitalism will not necessarily mean the end of every managerial oppression the capitalists have created. What do you think would be needed to undo this legacy?

Further Reading

Light

In Praise of the Dancing Body, an essay Silvia Federici wrote for Gods&Radicals: https://abeautifulresistance.org/site/2016/08/22/in-praise-of-the-dancing-body

The 100% True Story of the Writing of the Communist Manifesto (an Existential Comic): http://existentialcomics.com/comic/203

("hobgoblin," by the way, comes from a hilarious mistranslation of *The Communist Manifesto* which begins, "There's a frightful hobgoblin vexing Europe, the hobgoblin of Communism...")

Moderate:

Wages Against Housework, a manifesto from Silvia Federici written in the late 70's. https://caringlabor.wordpress.com/2010/09/15/silvia-federici-wages-against-housework/

Intensive

The Marxist program of the Black Panther party, from one of its co-founders, Huey P. Newton,
https://www.marxists.org/history/usa/workers/black-panthers/1966/10/15.htm

CHAPTER FIVE: What Can We Do?

In the previous four chapters we looked at how capitalism works, how it came about, how it exploits us and how it manages our relations to each other. In this final chapter, we'll look at what Marx and others suggested we do it about it, how we can fight it and what we might build instead.

The Capitalists Have Won...

Perhaps at this point it seems that any resistance to the capitalists is futile. We have behind us hundreds of years of systematic oppression, racial and gender divisions, and powerful governments with militaries and police forces ready to prevent any uprising anywhere in the world.

What can possibly be done? How can we hope to undo these legacies, especially since we've seen that so many previous attempts to end capitalism have failed?

When Marx wrote *Capital*, he lived in a similarly depressing age. Marx himself was constantly on the run, fleeing to city after city because the capitalists of that era convinced kings and rulers to eject him from their lands. Journals he started were made illegal and printings seized by the police, and the manuscripts often had to be smuggled to printers (a problem faced by many other political radicals during that time).

We currently face no such dangers. It's incredibly unlikely

that anyone will censor this book, seize all copies of it, and force me to leave the city where I live because they consider these ideas too dangerous.

On the surface, the fact that we don't have to worry about censorship or arrest may seem like our modern age is more free. A darker reality is more likely, however: the capitalists no longer see Marx and his ideas as a threat.

In their mind, they've won, at least in the so-called Democratic nations of the world. No significant challenges to the power of capitalism have occurred in the United States for at least half a century. The awful failures of state-communism (the Soviet Union, the "Eastern Bloc" of communist states in Europe) has made many declare that the age of Marx is over. Marxist movements in Central and South America have been repeatedly crushed (usually by U.S. military intervention), and anywhere Marxist ideas re-appear in the minds of the people, those ideas are swiftly beaten out of them.

Marx's analysis may have been correct, but thus far nobody's been able to make any proposed alternative to capitalism succeed. On the one hand, we've seen totalitarian governments arise under the banner of "the worker" and subsequently reproduce all the terrors of capitalism; on the other, Marxist groups such as the Black Panthers in the United States lost their leaders to assassinations and imprisonment while being infiltrated by the FBI.

It would seem that capitalism can never be stopped.

...But another world is still possible.

Recall, though, what we learned in chapter three about the two ways of looking at history.

In the capitalist Progress Narrative, the present has killed the past. Everything that came before this moment was supposedly weaker, primitive, unenlightened, and we now live in a better time that can only ever get better. In the Progress Narrative, Marx's ideas belong in the trash can of history, along with all those other ideas we held in the past: animism, Paganism, indigenous customs, respect for nature, and ways of living where the market did not dominate every part of life. If the Progress Narrative is correct, than indeed Marxism has failed and should be forgotten.

On the other hand, if the Process Narrative is correct, than just like everything else that humans have ever struggled for, a life without capitalism is not only possible but probably inevitable. No empire has lasted forever, nor has any economic system been able to dominate the world for more than a handful of centuries. Old ways of thinking and being never fully go away: they persist as processes, as "presences," and not just in the dusty tomes of history. If the Process Narrative of history is correct, than there is still hope for us, still reason to fight and to struggle.

CAPITALISM & INTERNAL CONTRADICTIONS
Marx was especially good at analyzing capitalism on a system-basis to find where it was weakest. These "contradictions" can be seen as weak links or loose foundations in the capitalist system, and communists and others have often pushed to put pressure on these weak points so the system will collapse.

The Contradictions of Capital

What does Climate Change, the outsourcing of labor to cheaply-bought workers in the Global South, the housing and banking collapses at the end of the last decade, Brexit, and the current military tensions over Syria all have in common?

They're all crises caused by the contradictions of capital.

In the Marxist understanding of history, capitalism is created by processes and is itself a process that constantly destroys the natural world. As a process, however, capitalism has certain internal contradictions that are always threatening to end its reign, contradictions which always lead to crises.

Marx identified several such contradictions.

• The first is that the profit of capitalists is always limited by

97

the wages being paid to workers on both the upper end and the lower end.

• The second, which is tied to the first, is that there are "natural" limits on consumption and natural resources: workers can only consume so much stuff before they cannot consume any more, and there are only so many raw materials in the world to make things from.

• And the third is that the constant drive to "revolutionize the means of production" creates a working class with increased access to the means of revolt.

Each of these contradictions results in a crisis for capitalism, and Marx stated that it's in those points of crisis that capitalism can be destroyed.

Let's first look at each of these contradictions, then each of the crises that result from them, and then talk about what we can do about it.

Contradiction #1: Wages vs. Profit

In order to accumulate more wealth (capital), the rich need to buy labor from the working classes to transform raw material into products that can then be sold for consumption. This is as true for a farm owner and factory owner as it is for a restaurant owner or a tech company. Whether it's vegetables, cars, dinners, or smart phone applications, the imperative of the capitalist is to sell what workers produce.

Who does the capitalist sell those things to, though? Why, to workers of course—people being employed by capitalists to produce for them. This fact creates an uncomfortable problem for the capitalist class, because **in order to earn profit from the lower classes, the lower classes need to be making enough money to buy those products in the first place.**

A capitalist needs to reduce labor costs (wages) to the lowest rate possible in order to profit from a worker's production. At the high end, capitalists can never pay workers as much money as they sell all their production for, otherwise there's no profit.

What Can We Do?

However, if capitalists as a class (not just a few individual capitalists) pay workers less than they are selling their production for, than not all of the products they sell can be bought.

To understand exactly how this works, let's imagine an isolated village with 21 people. They don't trade or exchange with other villages, so their production and consumption occurs within a closed system.

Of the 21 people in the village, 1 of them (let's call her Becky) owns all the land and employs the other 20 to grow vegetables. That person, the capitalist, pays each of those people a wage of $1 a year, meaning that he or she pays a total of $20 in wages every year.

Assuming there are no other capitalists, and no one has any savings, there is now a total of $20 distributed in the pockets of the workers of the village. Becky needs to make up the money she spent on wages, and she needs to do so by selling the vegetables all the workers grew for her. And she also wants to make $1 in profit (Becky's not yet a very greedy capitalist).

TOTAL WAGES PAID TO WORKERS:
$20
MAXIMUM REVENUE FROM THOSE WORKERS AS CONSUMERS:
$20
MAXIMUM PROFIT POSSIBLE: $0

Do you see the problem? If there's only a total of $20 in circulation in the village, the most she can possibly get back from the workers is $20. There's literally no more money than that in the village.

Becky can't profit merely by selling what the workers produced back to them, because she can't raise the prices beyond the amount of money available. But also, Becky can't profit by reducing the wages she pays to the workers, because that reduces the amount of money they have to buy her products.

If she paid her workers half as much, then there would only

be half as much money for them to buy her products. Again, no profits.

There are only two ways she can increase her profits in such a situation, but both are only short-term tricks that postpone the inevitable.

Trick #1: Displace the Problem by Expanding

The first is to displace the problem by finding another village to sell her vegetables in. And let's say such a village exists: there are 20 workers there who each have a dollar in their pockets from wages they were getting from their own village capitalist (let's name him Bob). So if she sells her vegetables to just one of them, she's finally earned her $1 profit.

Bob, the second village's capitalist, has the same arrangement as Becky. He pays his workers $1 a year to grow vegetables and also wants $1 in profit. But now that Becky has taken one of those dollars away from him so she can profit, Bob can only get back $19 from the workers in the second village. Not only does he not profit, but he also loses $1, which means the next year he can only pay a maximum of $19 in wages.

This reduces the amount of money in circulation. If Becky continues to displace her problem by selling her extra vegetables to this second village, she can keep profiting for quite a few years. But eventually she will fully deplete their money supply. She'll be back in the situation she started in, and Bob will be out of business.

That is, she's only displaced the problem by expanding into another market, but eventually that market reaches the same limit as the first.

CAPITALIST EXPANSION AND "DEVELOPING MARKETS" Because capitalists require constant expansion in order to sustain their profit, they are constantly attempting to "develop" new markets, especially in the Global South. In every case, this means finding new consumers for their goods by destroying local businesses and local economies.

Trick #2: Manipulate Currency

There's another short-term fix: manipulating the value of currency so that the apparent amount in the village is always a little more than what the capitalist is paying them in wages. Imagine an extra 1 dollar suddenly appearing in the one of the pockets of one of the workers in the village. Now, there's $21 dollar in the village, and if the workers spend all their money on Becky's vegetables, she can have her profit. But how do you make 1 dollar magically appear in someone's pocket out of nowhere?

Credit is one way of increasing the circulation of money outside of wages and the sales of products. Individuals borrow money from a bank with the promise to pay back more than they borrowed at a later date, and they then use this borrowed money to purchase things the capitalists sell them. That means that the money the banks are lending to workers is actually going to the capitalists, since the workers eventually spend the money they borrowed. But of course, the capitalist isn't responsible for paying that money back, the workers are. And the only way for them to pay that money back is through their wages.

The problem here is that credit doesn't actually increase the amount of wealth in the village. In fact, it decreases the value of currency ("inflation"), so that the $1 a villager gets paid by the capitalist will buy them a little less each year. That's because the village capitalist will increase the cost of vegetables (because she wants to make at least $1 a year) while keeping the wages she

LOANS & MORTGAGES

When a person borrows money from a bank to buy a car or house, it's the bank who pays the seller. If banks didn't do this, sellers would be forced to accept lower prices for houses and cars (since very few people have that much money in their pocket). That means that banks are helping to inflate prices and ensure capitalists earn high rates of profit.

pays her workers the same. So the workers will never be able to pay that credit back, and the bankers will need to offer more credit to keep capitalists profiting.

Banks aren't the only ones who do this, by the way. Governments create currency through a similar process, and all that money they "create" eventually goes to the capitalists. But they aren't actually increasing the wealth in a society, only the amount of times that wealth circulates before ending up in the hands of the capitalists.

Contradiction #2: Finite Resources and the Concentration of Wealth

The villages in this example were both closed systems. That is, they were not engaged in trade or exchange with the rest of the world. Even when Becky from the first village began selling her vegetables to the workers in the second village, the two villages remained in a closed system together.

As we saw in the example of the two villages, when Becky started selling her vegetables in the second village, she was able to increase her profits temporarily by taking away Bob's potential profit and pulling wealth out of the second village. If Bob doesn't try to expand into Becky's village and cannot stop her from competing with him, eventually he'll run out of money to pay his workers, and they'll run out of money to buy her vegetables.

The only way for them to both profit is to find a third village and compete there, and then a fourth and fifth and so on until they've brought the entire world into their market economy. But at that point, there's nowhere else to expand.

And that's the key to the second contradiction of Capitalism: **the amount of consumers available for the products the capitalists want to sell them is finite.** The earth is a closed system; there are no malls on Jupiter where aliens flock every weekend to buy things made by workers on earth.

What Can We Do?

In those two villages, if Becky succeeded in conquering the "market" of the second village, Bob eventually runs out of money. That means he's got no more capital anymore (Becky has it all now!) and he's out of business. But that also means the workers in the second village aren't getting a wage from Bob anymore, so unless Becky hires them, they can't buy Becky's vegetables anymore.

If Becky wants the people in the second village to keep buying her vegetables, she needs to hire them to grow vegetables for her. But that puts her right back to where she started, and now she must yet again expand to another village, and then another, successfully wiping out each capitalist she competes with.

As she does this, Becky gets richer and richer: the wealth of all those villages is now increasingly concentrated into her hands. At the very same time, though, the amount of workers she relies upon to sell her vegetables increases too. But since there are fewer and fewer capitalists to pay wages to those workers (she eliminated them, remember), she has to rely more and more on expansion to keep her rate of profit.

But eventually, Becky will reach the last village and the last capitalist. When she puts that last capitalist out of business, there's nothing left. She "won," but she's also deeply lost. Because now the closed-loop system of wages and consumption finally kicks in; there are no more tricks to play, no more new markets to conquer.

Have hope: we're in that situation now.

When we hear studies reporting that 8 people hold 80% of the world's wealth, this is what that means. A handful of individuals

OIL, COAL, & CAPITALISM Entire books can have been written on the relationship between petrofuels and capitalist growth. Coal & oil provide extreme amounts of energy, and thus helped to give the impression that capitalism could expand infinitely. But we're running out of both and destroying the planet with emissions. Nothing lasts forever...

have conquered most of the villages of the world, and they're running out. They are reaching the limit of expansion, and as they get closer and closer to that limit, the amount of poor people in the world also reaches a crucial limit.

Soon we'll have no more money to buy what they have to sell, and as the massive financial sector collapses in the past decade have shown, the system of credit that temporarily increases the available currency we have is also reaching its limit.

Contradiction #3: The Revolution of Production Creates a Revolutionary Working-Class.

This text is a perfect example of the third contradiction of capitalism. It's an anti-capitalist book written on a computer produced through capitalism, printed on paper manufactured by capitalists, and distributed through networks owned by capitalists.

Now, remember: capitalists didn't actually create this book or any of those other things: workers did. Every single one of these things was and is possible without capitalism. But as capitalists push workers to produce more and more things for them to sell, those workers end up producing the means by which workers can liberate themselves from the capitalists, including this text.

Marx believed that, **by organizing the labor-power of humans, the capitalists were creating their own downfall**, a downfall that could only come about if the poor of the world—who are producing everything—finally noticed that it was their labor that made the world work. This "class consciousness" would be the first step to a revolution of workers against the capitalists. If that consciousness were ever attained, then the revolution would occur through the very things the workers were producing for the capitalists.

Imagine a weapons factory, owned by a capitalist who hires a hundred people to make guns and bullets for him. The hundred people who make those guns are literally producing the very thing that could be used for revolution, but only if those workers ever understood the power of the guns they were making and realised they could use them together against the owner.

The same is true for everything else workers produce for the capitalists. Migrant farmers who work the land for a large agribusiness are producing food they could eat and distribute to others, women in sweatshops are making clothing for the capitalists that they could instead wear and give to others. Internet engineers are making applications for corporations they could instead be making for others, and doctors and cooks are providing services that they could instead offer directly to other workers rather than for restaurants or corporate healthcare.

In order to harness more and more specialized labor, capitalists organize workers in a way that is incredibly dangerous for those capitalists. The accountant they hire to do their books, the managers they hire to lock up the shop at night, the internet engineers who design the operations programs for Google servers—much of the work for which capitalists buy our labor gives us shocking amounts of knowledge, access, and power over the capitalists. In fact, capitalists cannot employ labor without giving workers access to this power, otherwise there would be no way for workers to apply their labor to capital. But in granting access to this power, the capitalists are constantly risking their own demise.

One of the most crucial risks capitalists take is organizing

RECUPERATION
The relationship between workers and capitalists is very much a cat & mouse game. When workers come up with revolutionary ideas or ways to share resources, the capitalists attempt to assimiliate these back into capitalism. A good example is the "digital commons," file-sharing, and many other early internet technologies that capitalists quickly shut down. This is called recuperation, and it happens for ideas and symbols, too.

workers in a way where they start communicating with each other. Just as the plots of slave and serf revolts were often discussed in the fields of the lords or owners, strikes and sabotage are often discussed in factories or shops or restaurants while workers are working together on the property of the capitalist. The internet is another example of this: every part of it is owned by capitalists, yet it creates a means by which workers can communicate their anti-capitalist desires to each other.

Ceridwen's Chase

An important aspect of the Process Narrative (or specifically Historical Materialism) that I haven't quite mentioned yet is this: contradictions always seek resolution. But rather than give you the rather boring and not very clear Marxist explanation, there's a Welsh story that illustrates this point better: the story of Ceridwen and Taliesin.

Ceridwen had two children. The first of them was beautiful, the second was ugly and malformed. She loved them both, but grieved for how tormented the ugly child was by his deformities, so she sought to give him wisdom so he had something as powerful as beauty.

After consulting with ancient alchemists, she learned of a potion which, after brewed for a year and a day, would give a person the wisdom she sought. Unable to stir the potion herself all year, she asked a boy and an old man to look after it for her, and they agreed.

A year and a day passed, and the potion was almost ready. But the boy who minded the pot managed to "accidentally" get three drops of the brew on his tongue, and all the wisdom meant to go to Ceridwen's crippled child went to this boy instead. Realising she would be furious, the boy fled, using this stolen wisdom to shapeshift into other things so she could not find him. Ceridwen was a witch, though, and also shapeshifted, changing into something that could catch the form the thief had adopted.

So the chase lasted for a very long time, but eventually the boy changed into a seed that Ceridwen as a hen ate. That seed, though, grew inside her as a pregnancy until she bore a child: the same one who had stolen wisdom from her. And this time, because he was now her child, she did not kill him but merely sent him down a river in a sack to be raised by others.

The shape-shifting chase between Ceridwen (a goddess of wisdom, beauty, and death) and the boy (named Taliesin) describes how Marx saw the contradictions of capitalism. As Taliesin sought to flee his inevitable demise, he sought more and more "innovations" to escape, but then a crisis would occur: Ceridwen would shift form, become the very thing that could finally catch him. Capital (all the stolen wealth derived from our labor) constantly shifts form, tries to find a new way to escape the inevitability of justice. At some point, there will be no more possible shapeshifts to escape these crises, and Capital will be consumed by the people it was stolen from.

When Marxists say the end of capitalism is "inevitable," they don't mean it the way Christians say that Jesus's return is inevitable. Instead, they mean that capital is a contradiction seeking resolution, and in the crisis points it creates are the key to its end.

Let's look at those points of crisis.

Crisis #1: Currency and Debt

The primary method used to maintain a constant supply of consumers is the manipulation of currency through credit and central (governmental) banking agencies. In

NATURE & NATURAL LIMITS Welsh and other myths are full of similar stories where magicians and even gods attempt to circumvent the will of nature gods But in the early days of capitalism, engineers and scientists boasted of being conquerors of nature (and some even used rape metaphors in these boasts). But just as in those myths, nature's revolt against such arrogance in the form of Climate Change, extrinction, and resource depletion now reminds us that nature can only be pushed so far.

the United States, the treasury prints and destroys currency at a carefully controlled rate in order to ensure the money supply in the economy always increases but never by so much that inflation causes the economy to collapse.

If you are familiar with what happened in Weimar Berlin before the Nazis took power, you'll understand how careful they have to be about this. Runaway inflation can make a government topple in a matter of weeks or even days, because governments use currency to pay the soldiers and police who maintain the system and stop internal threats.

Manipulation of the currency supply ensures there is always a little extra "wealth" to be paid to the capitalists each year, but that wealth is not tied to anything actually real. That is, there's nothing behind currency except faith that the governments that issue them will always make sure they have value.

The credit system is even more fragile. In 2008 and 2009, a near global collapse of the world's economies occurred because of banks lending massive amounts of money to people in order to buy homes. With so much credit suddenly flooding the system, more people started buying homes which then caused the prices of homes to inflate. Speculators (those who buy things with the sole intention of reselling them at a higher rate in the near future) bought houses at even higher rates than workers, and when they all began reselling the homes at once the market in houses collapsed.

Millions of people lost money and homes, multinational banks collapsed or were "bailed out" by governments, and capitalists fired workers in droves. Workers without wages

MARKET COLLAPSE
Markets are said to collapse when most sellers can no longer make a profit from their product and are forced to sell at a loss. However, in most cases these collapses occure because prices were artificially inflated previously by speculation by investors (as in the housing collapse of 2008-2009).

can't buy things, though, which meant capitalists began losing money on sales, which caused them to fire more workers, which then...you get the point.

Only the intervention of governments who "bought up" the debt from the banks and corporations stopped this crisis, but it didn't stop the underlying problem. Other stop-gaps were also put in place, including a system that will temporarily shut down trading on stock exchanges if it appears that another such crisis is occurring. That is: the economy will still collapse, but the rich will have a little more warning.

Crisis point #2: War and Climate Change

The second contradiction of capitalism, in which there is only a finite amount of wealth to be had for the capitalists and that capitalism always leads to a concentration of wealth in the hands of a few, leads to a crisis that Marx only partially foresaw.

Marx understood that the finite nature of the earth would lead to the "declining rate of profit," that eventually it would be harder and harder for capitalists to extract more wealth in the form of resources and labor from people and the planet. But what neither he nor the capitalists of that time could see was that the extraction of resources from the earth and the waste from industrial capitalist production would eventually trigger an environmental crisis, too.

The earth is a closed system. When carbon dioxide and other greenhouse gases are released through production in factories (including coal power plants) and consumption (particularly combustion engines in automobiles), there's nowhere else for them to go.

Just as there are no malls on Jupiter where the capitalists of earth can sell their surplus products, there's no smokestack tall enough to vent out the excess CO_2 capitalism produces. Instead, it remains trapped in the atmosphere where it in turn traps sunlight which heats the earth, melts glaciers and ice caps, and wreaks utter havoc on all the living ecosystems to which humans are connected.

CHAPTER FIVE

Scientists often call this geologic age the "Anthropocene," meaning that it is the first in the history of the earth in which human activity has more affect on the earth than any other process or influence. Most environmental scientists, even those who are not necessarily critical of capitalism as a system, agree that the Anthropocene started with the birth of industrial capitalism in the mid-1700's.

Climate change is absolutely a crisis everyone faces, particularly the poor and those who live in the "Global South," where governments and people have fewer resources to combat the problems climate change causes. In chapter three we saw why those people and governments are poorer, and it's an even more tragic irony that the wealth extracted from them during colonization (primitive accumulation) became the wealth the capitalists used to cause global warming.

While it's a crisis for everyone, climate change is also a crisis for the capitalists themselves. As forests die off, groundwater, entire species, and arable land disappears, and as cities begin to flood from rising seas, the capitalists are having a harder time accumulating more capital.

A forest destroyed by disease, drought, or wildfire cannot be cut down for lumber to be sold to people for homes. As topsoil erodes and farming becomes impossible in more and more places, less food production is possible through capitalist means. Flooding and other weather-related disasters directly destroys factories, stores, homes, and other other things the capitalists use to earn more capital, as well as creating a deep instability in labor markets which makes it difficult for them to hire workers.

METABOLIC RIFT
Though he did not know about Global Warming, Marx did appear to understand and forsee climate change. His theory, called "Metabolic Rift," suggested that capitalism could not renew the resources it took from the earth (especially soil); this "rift" would eventually undermine capitalism,

What Can We Do?

There are now hundreds of security firms, perhaps thousands, which market their services to the rich with branded promises to help them "negotiate the challenges" of climate crisis (a crisis the rich themselves have created!) along with the other looming crisis caused by capitalism's contradictions: war, terrorism, and other global "insecurities."

War and capitalism have an uncomfortable relationship. On the one hand, war creates interruptions to markets. It's very difficult for capitalists to sell their products when bombs are falling, and it's likewise difficult to find labor when most workers are busy shooting other workers. In fact, if there is anything nice to say about capitalists, it's that their aversion to risk and unstable markets makes them less likely to support military conflicts where their ability to profit is threatened.

This risk aversion doesn't stop them from supporting wars, however, it just means they prefer wars against weaker countries. Thus, the capitalists in the United States and the United Kingdom had no qualms with the invasions of Afghanistan or Iraq, but are much less likely to support a war with each other or with Russia or China.

On the other hand, remember Becky and Bob? If Bob had built a wall around the village to keep Becky from selling her vegetables to his workers, Becky would hit the natural limit of profit early and go out of business. But if Becky hired a few of the villagers to destroy that wall and kill anyone trying to stop them, then Becky could sell her vegetables to Bob's workers and avoid her own demise.

War and conquest have always been the quickest (albeit expensive) way to accumulate capital. Invade a country, take their oil or gold or uranium, and you immediately have a lot more wealth you can then use as capital. But they are also good ways to "open up" closed markets for capitalists, and wars become a necessity when those capitalists are facing a crisis of profit.

So the contradiction between capitalists' need for endless growth and the finite nature of resources doesn't just result in the crisis of climate change, it also results in the crisis of war. Both war and climate change cause insecurity for the capitalists, potentially destroying their capital, causing them to lose access to markets, and most of all creating a labor crisis.

Aside: The October Revolution

Nowhere was this labor crisis seen best than in the Russian revolution of 1917, in which peasants and workers overthrew the Tsarist government of Russia. Inspired by the writings of Marx and anarchists such as Proudhon, that revolution is significant not just because of the communist state which replaced it (eventually an unfortunately totalitarian and oppressive one) but also because of its timing.

The global military conflict that started in Europe in 1914 drew in many nations (and their colonies), including Russia. Russian soldiers were the second largest military involved in the war, but in November of 1917 (or October, since Russia then used a different calendar), communists, socialists, anarchists, and others overthrew the government and effectively ended Russian participation in World War I. The war would continue for another year, but now with one side missing a quarter of its soldiers.

There are many reasons for the Russian revolution, but the war itself was undoubtedly a larger part of it. As we saw with pillaging and conquest, paying and feeding soldiers costs a lot of money. Not only are the direct costs of soldiers high, but when those soldiers would otherwise be workers producing food and other goods, the capitalists face profit loss. To make up for this loss during wars, capitalists and the governments that support them enact harsher productivity standards, reduce wages and benefits, and erase worker protections.

Increased exploitation of workers along with the costs of

maintaining an army caused a crisis in Russia which the revolutionaries were able to exploit. The government was weakened and had fewer police and soldiers at home to protect them while the capitalist class was severely hated. These two processes together meant that when workers rose up against both the government and the rich at once, they were able to get enough support from so many sections of the lower classes that the revolution succeeded.

Capitalists outside Russia learned an important lesson. During war they are particularly vulnerable from the workers they exploit. Governments also learned an important lesson: during war, repression of worker revolts from within the country are vital to the success of war outside the country. Thus, as the beginning of World War II, every nation (including the by then totalitarian U.S.S.R) immediately arrested dissidents, anarchists, pacifists, and foreigners who might cause instability.

Crisis Point #3: Us.

The final point of crisis caused by the contradictions of capitalism has already been discussed in some detail: the constant "revolutionizing" of the modes of production creates a working class increasingly capable of seizing the means of production for themselves.

When I was in my early 20's, revolution seemed inevitable. You can maybe forgive me this optimism. After all, I lived in Seattle, which had just seen a meeting of global bankers, CEOs, and world leaders shut down by 60,000 people dressed as sea turtles and fairies. Soon after were the massive protests at the G8 summits in Europe, the beginning of the World Social Forum in South America, and man-ifestations against the conventions of both the Republican and Democratic National Conventions against which the US government deployed tanks.

Independent media collectives sprung up in every major city of the world, new co-operatives and skill shares and solidarity networks were birthed and spread and communicated with each other across the vast distances of oceans and cultures, and I and everyone I knew could say along with Arundhati Roy,

> "Another world is not only possible, but she is on her way. On a still day, I can hear her breathing."

Two decades ago, the world seemed on the brink of a revolution that would finally end capitalism and its endless destruction of the environment and people. And yet here we are now, in 2019, a small handful of us discussing the Marxist anti-capitalist framework and wondering whether it's even still relevant.

It's difficult to even imagine another world when we look at the world around us now. Increased surveillance, exploding prison populations, police murders of unarmed people of color, massive refugee crises, and military occupations in the Middle East with threats of more war on the horizon.

All of this, along with an increasing concentration of wealth in the hands of a very few, widespread precarious employment where people work multiple jobs online for decreasing pay, the closure of factories and physical manufacturing moved to cheaper labor markets, and fascist, white supremacist, and other ultra-nationalist movements marching through streets attacking immigrants and activists with impunity.

That "other world" seems awfully far away now, less than two decades after the time we all thought she would arrive any moment. The thing is, the world actually was on the brink of anti-capitalist revolution, and we are now living in a capitalist counter-revolution.

Recall how, in the Process Narrative, the events of human history occur not as a linear progression but as a conflict of forces, processes, and actions. Using this framework instead of the capitalist Progress Narrative, we have every reason to suspect that the massive militarization of police forces and increase in government repression of dissent around the world is a reaction.

Something had the rich and powerful worried enough to invest their capital in tools of oppression, violence, and control, and that something was us.

Think like a capitalist for a moment, and imagine the fear that would have struck into your soul as you watched leaders of capitalist nations cowering in hotel rooms as 60,000 people shouted and sang and chanted demands that they stop exploiting people. Imagine the catch in the throat as you heard cities and governments had to deploy troops through the commercial districts of "modern" capitalist cities in Europe and the United States to stop people from smashing the windows of Starbucks and Nike.

Imagine the anxiety hearing that indigenous movements in South America had successfully claimed control of their governments and natural resources as factories were shut down or burned to the ground in the cheap labor markets of Southeast Asia.

GLOBALIZATION
In response to several massive financial crises in the 1970's, many governments of the world began to weaken their restrictions on the movement of capital in and out of their nations. This resulted in several trade agreements which favored capitalists over workers and re- duced local gov- ernment control of economies. This process was called "globaliza- tion," and led to the rise of inter- national corpora- tions, job outsourcing, so- cial upheaval, and an exponential increase in environmental destruction across the globe.

Imagine what it must have been like to overhear people wherever you went, whether they were your employees or the servers at the restaurants where you ate or the clerks at the boutiques where you shopped talking about you, you and people like you, and they had nothing good to say about you.

Wherever you went or whatever you watched, you heard

about climate change, or over-consumption, or anarchists, or riots, or revolution.

Think like a capitalist or a politician, imagine what it must have been like to feel like the world was turning against you, and ask, "what would I do?"

The answer to that question is all around us, the capitalist counter-revolution I mentioned. This is how they stopped us, how they dealt with the crisis that comes from the third contradiction of capitalism. By employing our labor to profit from their capital, they had inadvertently given us the means to liberate ourselves from their rule. Just like a slave with a machete or factory workers in a gun factory, we held in our hands the weapons we could use to free ourselves.

The capitalists, terrified, saw this and acted against us. New systems of oppression, new surveillance methods, stronger police and security forces, tighter control on the media and communications networks—these are just some of the ways they've used to prevent us from birthing a world where they can no longer profit from our labor.

History doesn't repeat itself, but it is full of repeating forms. The processes and contradictions which bring capitalism to its crisis points won't go away just because the capitalists try to stop them. Like opiates, these measures only suppress the symptoms and dull the pain, pain which exists to warn them there is something very wrong that needs to be addressed.

Communism

Marxism is communism, but until this point we haven't looked at what communism is about. I've saved this for the very end of the text specifically because it, more than anything else, is what I hope you take away from my words.

Communism, simply stated, is a system in which workers collectively own all the means of their own production and distribute all labor and goods according to the principle,

"from each according to their ability, to each according to their need."
Communism can be more than that, but it cannot be less than that. Economic and political systems which give workers only partial ownership of the means of production (for instance, nations where some industries are privately-owned and others are nationalised) are not communist. They may be socialist, or "democratic socialist," but unless all production is in the hands of those who actually do the production, such societies are still capitalist.

Likewise, nations which "socialize" certain costs (such as universal health care, welfare, universal basic income, or free universities) while still protecting the interests of capitalists (for instance, places like Sweden or France) are also still capitalist.

Communism requires complete control of production and labor by the workers for a very simple reason: anything short of this still allows capitalists to exploit people.

In fact, the governments of socialist countries are actually more protective of the long-term interests of capital than places like the United States. This is because the governments in such countries reduce the costs capitalists incur in their pursuit of profit.

Examples of how this works include:

• Universal health care helps the capitalists always have a healthy and productive work-force.

• Universal basic income, an idea heavily touted by free-market libertarians, frees a capitalist from ever worrying workers will be unable to buy their products.

• Free universal higher education creates a trained and specialized labor force for the capitalists to exploit.

• State-funded welfare programs provide temporary relief from the damage capitalists cause to the poor through gentrification, displacement, and other shifts in capital, but do not actually end the damage.

• Even state-funded public transportation systems help the

capitalists, by increasing the geographical area from which they can draw the labor they need to increase their capital.

Each of things are "good" things. Combined together, they create societies which are safer, more stable, and more pleasant to live in than hyper-capitalist nations like the United States. But no matter how much each of these social programs are applied, they can never solve the root problems caused by capitalism.

Also, there is a darker side to these partial-socialist societies which few ever like to admit. While they are better places to live than the United States, the prosperity, comfort, and higher standards of living in places such as France or Sweden are ultimately paid for by the labor and suffering of poorer nations. France, where I live now, was a colonialist power, and many of the beautiful places I walk through in this city were built from stolen African wealth. It is the same in all European cities, just as it is in every other "progressive," "socialist," or "liberal" city in the world.

Communism stops this oppression, because it insists **all workers, everywhere, must own the means of their own production and must be the ones who decide how to distribute the wealth they create.** This means that the women sewing t-shirts in Bangladesh, the children mining coltan in Africa, the workers assembling iPhones in Chinese factories, and the Mexicans picking vegetables under the sweltering Texas or Californian sun must be the ones who decide what is done with the goods they produce, not "the market" or capitalists exploiting their labor.

To get to such a point, we would need a revolution everywhere, not just in one city or a few countries. Because as long as some capitalists continue to be capitalists, their imperative to expand to find new markets in which to sell and new sources of labor and resources to exploit will threaten the lives of the entire planet with war and climate change.

Autonomous Marxism vs. Totalitarian Communism.

All Marxists agree on these points. Most anarchists do, as well. Where everyone diverges, however, is exactly how to implement such a revolution.

For instance, Lenin, Trotsky, and Stalin all believed that seizing control of the government and using it to implement Marxist policies was the only way to fend off threats from capitalists within and without. The legacy of their attempts to do this were catastrophic. The U.S.S.R. quickly shifted from a collection of local communist councils into a totalitarian behemoth which imprisoned and murdered other Marxists who even slightly disagreed with their vision. China (which originally followed much of the Leninist program) has morphed into a massive industrial capitalist state even more totalitarian than the Soviet Union ever got.

Other interpretations of Marxist theory into practice completely avoid totalitarian tendencies and oppose any attempt to seize control of the capitalist state. For instance, the revolutionary program of the Black Panthers called for the state's dissolution and demanded all authority be put into the hands of local groups who were involved in the matters at hand.

This latter interpretation is called "**Autonomous Marxism**," or sometimes also "Libertarian Communism" or "Anarcho-Communism." In the views of those who hold these ideologies, any attempt of a larger group to control the actions of smaller groups repeats the same exploitation of capitalism. More so, many indigenous Marxist movements have followed these ideologies.

Autonomous Pagan Marxism

This text has been an introduction to Marxism, and I hope by now you feel you've a comfortable grip on what Marxism is about. But this text can't start a revolution, nor can I. But **we** can start one. And we'll need lots of help.

The first step to any revolution is for the people who are oppressed and exploited to see each other as a collective class with mutual interests. This is true whether we are talking about Black liberation or women's liberation or anti-capitalist revolt. But the best anti-capitalist revolt, and in my mind the only possible anti-capitalist revolution, would also seek the liberation of women and Black folks and any other group exploited by the capitalists.

Key to creating this solidarity is also rejecting the mechanistic worldview that the capitalists have foisted upon us. Many Marxists and Anarchists unfortunately accept Calvinist views on nature, animism, and religious beliefs, believing that Pagan and indigenous ways of seeing the world are "backwards" or "primitive." The acceptance of this worldview has meant that First Nations and other colonized peoples have been belittled or expected to reject their ancestral cultures in order to become revolutionary.

AUTONOMOUS MARXISM
A system of Marxism that advocates small-scale community control of local resources and labor, rather than large-scale party-led central control.

Once enough people understand that their oppression is tied up in others' oppression, class consciousness can arise. From the consciousness we can build power, organizing together against exploitation and begin "seizing the means of production."

Seizing the means of production can be as simple as reclaiming land for gardening and farming, but it must be enough to begin supporting people outside of capitalist modes of production. "Local Food" movements, Community-Supported Agriculture, community gardens, and food co-ops are all starts to this process.

Seizing the means of production, though, involves much more, including taking over restaurants, factories, power plants, shops, and many other places controlled by the capitalists. At this point, a Pagan Marxism begins to diverge from many other urban versions of Autonomous Marxism.

Most Marxists imagine we need to take over everything that the capitalists own now and keep up the same levels of production (this was Lenin's fatal error). Capitalism produces a lot of stuff we don't need, and the capitalists spend trillions of dollars on advertizing to make us think we need it. Not only do we not need all this, but we probably don't even want it.

The earth can't afford it either. Capitalism has caused a crisis of the climate, and destroying the planet in a more communist way instead of capitalist means we'll all die anyway.

This means that there's actually a lot less for us to seize than it seems like, which makes the potential for a communist revolution much more possible.

And we don't need to start the revolution everywhere all at once. It can start in a few places and spread, but it will have to spread faster than the capitalists can fight it, while also building enough of an alternative that can withstand any counter-revolutionary tactics. This is called "dual-power" strategy: creating organisational structures which compete with capitalist systems while forcing capitalism into crises.

What happens after that? Violence, most likely. Capitalists don't like losing their capital, and have repeatedly shown themselves willing to hire people with guns to stop any threat. They also rely on those people forgetting they are workers like us, and on us being so terrified of those hired guns that we don't confront them.

DO REVOLUTIONS HAVE TO BE VIOLENT?

Taking control of the resources needed to reate our own cthings for our own ends, rather than for the profit of capitalists, doesn't have to mean violence. Unfortunately, in many cases it may lead to violence if police, soldiers, and hired security guards try to stop workers. One way to lessen this possibility is to convince the people paid to protect the capitalists to join us instead.

And after that? If we win, we get to live for ourselves again, using our labor as we see fit, giving it to others according to their need.

And if we lose, then we'll try again. As Ursula K. Le Guin said:

> We live in capitalism. Its power seems inescapable. So did the divine right of kings. Any human power can be resisted and changed by human beings.

Study Questions & Further Reading

1. A lot of esoteric economic principles are covered in this chapter. Try to briefly explain the three contradictions of capitalism in your own words

2. Debt is not just a trick to keep the economy going, it's also been used throughout history as a way of pushing people into slavery (indentured servanthood and debtors prisons, for instance). Try translating the amount of debt you currently owe into work hours. How many hours will you have to work just to pay banks or other creditors?

3. Capitalist displacement of crises is often geographical. For instance, the off-shoring of manufacturing from Europe and the United States to the Global South was a way of displacing environmental destruction into countries with more complicit governments and counter-acting strong labor movements in those original countries. What other ways do you think capitalists merely move their crises around the globe?

4. If you work for an employer, think about the ways that you have been given access to aspects of production that you take for granted.

5. How much of your daily life is reliant on purchasing services from other people? For instance, how often do you eat from restaurants rather than preparing your own food? Make a list of basic skills you currently rely on others for, and consider learning one of those skills.

6. "The Means of Production" starts with land. Look around your neighborhood for space where you or others might be able to grow food. And then look around for security cameras, fences, and other "Enclosures." How are the Commons physically enclosed around you? How often are the Enclosures in your mind?

Further Reading

Light:

"Mad Marx," an Existential Comic: http://existential-comics.com/comic/186

Solidarity Networks, a guide to organizing with your friends based on communist principles
https://abeautifulresistance.org/site/2016/11/12/solidarity-networks

Moderate:

Anthropologist and Anarchist David Graeber's essay on how technological innovation and capitalism don't really go together. *On Flying Cars and the Declining Rate of Profit*: https://thebaffler.com/salvos/of-flying-cars-and-the-declining-rate-of-profit

Intensive:

The Climate of History, by Dipesh Chakrabarty, an essay examining the Anthropocene as a crisis not just for capitalism but for the societies built upon them:
https://godsandradicals.files.wordpress.com/2018/04/chakrabarty_2009.pdf

Important Terms

Alienation of Labor: The feeling of not being connected to your labor. Under capitalism, humans do not get to experience the direct benefit of their labor and instead receive wages. This leads to the sense that labor is not something that is part of us, that we have no control over our creative powers, or even that labor is something that we can ever have control over.

Animism: the name for the beliefs of most tribal and indigenous peoples in the world (including pre-Monotheist Europe), as well as followers of Shinto, Paganism, and many other religions. In animism, all of material existence has spirit and there is no separation between "physical" and "spiritual."

Autonomous Marxism: A system of Marxism that advocates for small-scale community control of local resources and labor, rather than large-scale party-led central control.

(The) Black Death: The Bubonic Plague, a disease which spread initially through fleas carried by rats and then eventually through air. The Black Death killed between 30% and 60% of Europe's population, primarily in densely-populated areas. The societal breakdown it caused ironically helped the poor greatly: survivors fled manors and founded free towns, Pagan rites flourished in many places, and wages greatly increased as the rich had a harder time finding workers.

Bourgeoisie (owners) Those who profit from the work of others and do not need to work for a wage in order to survive. The word means "town dweller" in French, reflecting the birth of capitalism within the cities of Europe.

Calvinism: A Protestant version of Christianity founded by John Calvin. It teaches that God has predestined his chosen people and the wealth is a sign of God's favor. It also taught that hard work and a strict morality made you holy. The Puritans who colonized New England were Calvinists.

Capital: Wealth that is used to make more wealth. This can include money invested to build a factory or restaurant, or other investments ("finance capital"). Capital is not the same as money or wealth, but rather a way that money or wealth is used.

Capitalism: A way of organizing society in which a small group of people own most of the resources and the rest of the people have to work for them to gain access to those resources to survive

Chattel Slavery: The most severe form of slavery, in which the slave and their offspring are fully-owned by the slave owner. The transatlantic slave trade that brought African slaves to the America was chattel slavery. The word chattel comes from the same Latin word from which we have both the words cattle and capital.

Class: An arrangement of society where people are divided according to their position, status, or activity; for instance, nobles, clergy, and peasants; or warrior, priest, and farmer; or master and slave; or worker and owner.

Class Conflict: The tension between the working class and the capitalist class caused by their competing interests. Workers want the highest value possible from their labor and therefore high wages, while capitalists want the highest profit from their capital and therefore low wages.

Class Consciousness: When those of a class (either the working class or the capitalist class) set aside other differences to act together on their shared interests as part of a class. For workers this can mean setting aside other differences and going on strike; for capitalists, this often means colluding to lower wages and benefits to workers.

Colonization: Colonization is the conquest and settlement of foreign lands by a political power in order to extract wealth. Colonization isn't just settlement (mirgrants and refugees settle in new lands all the time). Instead, colonies are set up for the sole purpose of expanding political and economic power.

(The) Commons: Land and other resources that were shared among a community for their collective use. For instance, rivers for fishing, water, and bathing; forests for hunting, wood, and foraging, and meadows for grazing, growing food, and community events.

Consumption: The use of a thing, whether that destroys the thing or not. So food is consumed, but so too is art.

(The) Dark Ages: a term used to describe the period between the fall of Rome and the beginning of the Renaissance in Italy. It was named this way in the 1600's by a Christian theologian, Petrarch, who claimed there was no writing being done and no knowledge discovered during this period. This is in fact untrue, but most of the discoveries were being done by Pagans, Jews, and Muslims who didn't count in his estimation.

Division of Labor: The way that work is assigned to people according to race, class, gender, and physical or intangible characteristics. For instance, women are assigned emotional and domestic labor more often than men are. Immigrants are assigned more agricultural labor, poor males are assigned more manual and factory labor, etc..

Economics: The management of production, consumption, and transfers of wealth. From the ancient Greek work *oikonomia*, which referred to household management. It was introduced into Modern society through the Catholic Church, which believed there was a God-ordained way that societies should be managed.

Enclosure: The act of turning public land and other resources into private property.

(The) Enlightenment: Also called "The Age of Reason," the Enlightenment supposedly meant the end of the Dark Ages and the beginning of a new era of knowledge. But though many of our ideas about freedom and rights come from this period, many of the same thinkers who iterated them also advocated slavery, the colonization of foreign lands, racial ideology, and capitalism.

Feudalism: The dominant political and economic system in Europe between the ninth and fifteenth centuries. In feudalism, rich landowners (lords) supported stronger landowners (including kings) in return for military protection. Feudal lords controlled the peasant on their land and extracted a third of everything they produced in taxes. Those peasants were not allowed to leave the land or to marry without permission from the lord.

Globalization: an expansion of capitalism across national borders by international corporations and global finance groups. This process greatly weakened the ability of local resistance to fight capitalist exploitation directly, since corporations can now merely move their factories to cheaper labor markets.

Historical System: A system that can be traced to a specific time period and was created by historic forces. For capitalism, those historical forces were the enclosure of the commons in Europe and the accumulation of wealth through slavery and colonization of indigenous peoples in Africa, Asia, and the Americas.

Industrialization: A way of organizing and exploiting labor in which work is done in factories, mills, and other large-scale situations. In industrial capitalism, workers are treated like machines with only a few tasks they must repeat for hours on end.

Internal Contradictions: Points of conflict within a system where something necessary for its existence and perpetuation is limited by opposite conditions. For instance, the fact that capitalism requires infinite growth is contradicted by the finite nature of the earth.

Labor: Work that is applied to resources in order to create something from it. Labor is what transforms clay into pottery, ingredients into dinner, stone into a house, or knowledge into an essay.

Market Imperative: Under Capitalism, economic logic now dominates all other considerations (religious, traditional, civil, moral, environmental, etc..) that previously trumped the demand for profit. In capitalism, one need only look at climate change to see how profit now dominates over all other concerns, even the future of earth itself.

(The) Means of Production: The resources required to produce something. For instance, land, farming tools, water, and seeds are all needed to grow food, so all those things are the means of production of food.

(The) Mechanistic Worldview: The moral, intellectual, and ideological framework that arose with the birth of capitalism. In this worldview, the machine became the primary metaphor for life, nature, work, society, and even God. This worldview continues in the way we talk about ourselves as machines and computers (for instance, "having a breakdown" or "I need time to process that.")

Metabolic Rift: The Marxist observation that capitalist production is unable to renew the resources it exploits and essentially suffers a "rift" between nature and production.

Middle Class: A group of better-compensated working class people whose values are often closer to the bourgeoisie than to their fellow proletariat.

Noblesse Oblige: The informal system of rights and obligations of the rich under feudalism. Lords were bound to protect the serfs on their land, but also claimed certain rights (like the right to have sex with a serf on their wedding night). This system was upheld by custom, religion, and sometimes (in the case of obligations to serfs) by riot and violence from peasants.

Patriarchy: A political system in which men are given preferential treatment over women. Capitalism is a patriarchal system.

Political Relations: The ways the laws, governments, power, force, coercion, and violence influence what we do, what we cannot do, and how we interact with each other

Primitive Accumulation: The process of gaining wealth (often violently) in order to later use that wealth as capital. Slavery, colonialism, pillaging, and Enclosure are all forms of primitive accumulation. The word primitive in this case means "primary" or "initial" and doesn't have the negative connotation the capitalist Progress Narrative gives it.

Private Property: A system in which land and resources are property that can be bought or sold. For instance, under capitalism land is private, so only those who have money to buy land can raise their own food. Private Property does not refer to Personal Property (like clothing).

Privilege: A crucial part of capitalist management, privilege is any right or benefit given to one group of workers over another group. This can take many forms, but the important thing to remember is that privilege is a capitalist method of control, not an inherent trait.

Process Narrative: An animist and Marxist way of looking at the world and everything in it as things always in states of continual change and cycles. In this view, old and young, modern and primitive, and future and past are merely states of being, not value judgments.

Production: The creation of things by humans for consumption, use, exchange, or enjoyment, as well as the process by which those things are created.

Progress Narrative: The capitalist idea that human society is constantly getting better, becoming more advanced and more free. In this view, the past was "backwards" and "dark" while the future will inevitably be even better than the present.

Proletariat (workers): The lower class of capitalist society, those who must work for a wage in order to survive. This group also includes the homeless, disabled, retired, and others who cannot or do not work but have no independent wealth.

Race: A way of categorizing humans that arose with capitalism. In race, humans with certain characteristics (primarily skin color and geographical origin) are categorized differently than those with other characteristics.

Recuperation: The process by which capitalists and the state undermine and then absorb challenges to their power. For instance, environmentalist challenges to capitalism are recuperated when corporations label themselves "green" and claim to care about climate change.

Slavery: A system or condition of coerced labor where the worker receives no compensation and cannot easily escape the situation.

Social Relations: All the interactions human have with each other, how they relate to each other and how they see themselves as part of a social group

State: The government, including all its institutions, laws, and officials. So politicians, judges, police officers, tax officials, prisons, courts, the military, and all the laws they create and enforce. Capitalists rely on these laws and institutions to protect their interests.

Surplus Production: What is created above what the person who created it uses or needs. This extra is either shared or traded in exchange for the surplus of others. In capitalism, surplus production is the property of the capitalist, not the worker.

Transfer of Wealth: How wealth (in the form of money or resources) is moved from one person to another.

Value: What a thing is considered to be worth. The concept of value extends into the far Pagan past, when a thing or a person was said to have value because it reflected an aspect of the gods. Value was once thought to be intrinsic (inherent to a person or thing). In modern capitalism, however, value (be that they worth of a thing or a person) is determined by the market, by how much someone is willing to pay for it.

Wages: The price owners pay to purchase labor.

About the Author

Rhyd Wildermuth is a writer, theorist, poet, druid, and a pretty decent cook. His early life was in a coal-heated dilapidated house with an open sewer in the foothills of Applachia with only trees, stars, spirits, and books to give him hope for a better world. After raising his two younger sisters and finishing high-school, he moved first to one coast of the United States and then the other, becoming an activist and a punk while working in restaurants and later as a social worker.

Now, he's the publisher of Gods&Radicals Press, which he helped found. He lives with his husband in France, gardens, lifts weights, cooks for friends, and wanders ancient Pagan sites in the forests and villages near his home.

Find more of his personal writing at paganarch.com, or his other books at abeautifulresistance.org/rhyd-wildermuth

Gods&Radicals Press

Gods&Radicals Press is a not-for-profit anti-capitalist publisher and website, founded on Beltane, 2015. We publish works on Paganism, animism, anarchism, and Marxism, and distribute worldwide.

Find more of our publications at abeautifulresistance.org or write to us at distro@abeautifulresistance.com

CPSIA information can be obtained
at www.ICGtesting.com
Printed in the USA
LVHW050805050223
738643LV00007B/94